Soft Furnishings

MARSHALL CAVENDISH

© Marshall Cavendish Limited 1985, 1992

Produced by Marshall Cavendish Limited 1985, 1992.

Produced by Marshall Cavendish Books
(A division of Marshall Cavendish Partworks Limited)
119 Wardour Street, London W1V 3TD.

ISBN 1 85435 508 2

Printed in Singapore.

INTRODUCTION

There is a satisfaction in making soft furnishings which is quite unique. Whether it's a few colourful cushions to liven up a colour scheme, or a complete set of co-ordinating room furnishings, the impact of the items you've made nearly always outweighs the time and effort spent on them. In less time than it takes to make a dress, you can totally transform a window, piece of furniture, even an entire room.

As well as their immense decorative value, making a home brighter, cheerier and cozier, soft furnishings are also practical. If you can make your own duvet covers, curtains, loose covers and tablecloths, for example, you can save a small fortune—and you have the chance to suit them exactly to your own requirements.

One of the pleasures of working on soft furnishings is the anticipation of how nice the finished item will look. And, of course, fabric can be a delight to work with in itself, especially if you have chosen colours, patterns and/or textures you really like.

Yet it is precisely because soft furnishings *can* be quite dominant features of a room that it is so difficult to disguise any flaws. A shoddy job is a waste of time, of money—and of an opportunity to enhance a room. Yet achieving a professional finish is not difficult if you know exactly what to do. That is the purpose of this book, to show you, one step at a time, the right way to make the main soft furnishings: window treatments, bed linen, cushions and seating, and table linen. Surprisingly enough, the proper techniques are often the simplest, as well as the most rewarding. And once you've learned these skills, you'll be able to use the book again and again as a reference source, for adding a personal touch to whatever you make.

CONTENTS

CURTAINS & BLINDS
Perfect curtains

Lined or unlined curtains are simple to make if you follow our detailed instructions for choosing a heading, estimating quantities, cutting out the fabric and making up.

Although there are various ways of covering a window, curtains remain as popular and practical as ever.

For their first attempt at curtain making, most people choose unlined curtains. These are particularly suitable for kitchens as they are so easy to wash. Add linings and they shut out more light, hang better and provide greater insulation.

Traditionally, linings are an integral part of the curtain, but modern heading tapes allow you to add detachable linings. Detachable linings are especially useful since if they wear out, they can easily be renewed.

Choosing your heading tape

Curtain tapes are narrow strips of tough, durable fabric available by the metre in white, natural, and a very small range of colours. They have pockets for the curtain hooks which attach the tape to the curtain track and drawstrings which are pulled to form the curtain heading.

The heading tape you choose will determine the look of your curtains. Remember that, since different tapes gather the fabric to different degrees, some need more fabric than others.

It is important that the heading should match across the curtains. This is particularly important on triple- and cartridge-pleat tapes, where there is a wide gap between each group of pleats. Always begin by placing the heading tape to the curtain edge which will lie in the centre of the window, starting the tape in the middle of a pleat group.

Two special tapes are available for detachable linings to be used in conjunction with any decorative heading.

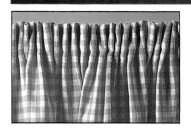

STANDARD AND CLUSTER PLEATS
Uses: Plain, so best hidden.
Fabric requirement: Even gathers — $1\frac{1}{2}$ times track length. Clusters — 2 times.
Fabric suitability: All weights.
Finish: Cheapest standard tape forms simple gathered headings only (left), but more expensive tape also forms clusters of shallow pleats (right). Tape for nets also available.

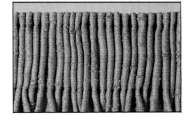

PENCIL PLEATS AND SPACED-PENCIL PLEATS
Uses: All types of unlined curtains, lined cotton and sheers. With track or pole.
Fabric requirements: $2\frac{1}{4}$-$2\frac{1}{2}$ times track length.
Fabric suitability: Fine fabric and cottons. Spaced pencil pleats on heavier fabrics (right).
Finish: Deep, crisp, evenly spaced pleats (left).

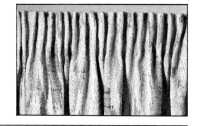

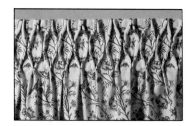

DECORATIVE HEADINGS
Uses: Shorter- and floor-length curtains. On valances, net and café curtains. For use on track or pole.
Fabric requirement: 2 times track length.
Fabric suitability: Cottons, medium-weight fabrics and sheers.
Finish: Traditional smocking, once achieved only by hand. Smocked (left) and Tudor (right).

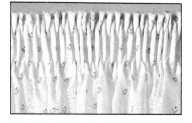

TRIPLE PLEATS
Uses: Radiator- and floor-length curtains. On track or pole.
Fabric requirement: 2 times track length.
Fabric suitability: All cottons and medium- to heavy-weight fabrics.
Finish: Either straight triple pleats (left) or fanned (right).

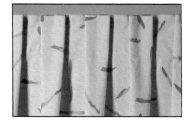

BOX-PLEAT AND CARTRIDGE TAPES
Uses: All types of curtains and sheers. Particularly good for thicker, lined curtains. Box-pleat tape can be used for valances.
Fabric requirements: 2-$2\frac{1}{2}$ times track length.
Fabric suitability: All weights of fabric.
Finish: Box pleat (left), cartridge pleats (right).

Working out quantities

Simply measure the length of one curtain plus turnings and seam allowances and multiply by the number of fabric widths

Example: If the length for one curtain is 190cm and you need 5 widths, then 190cm×5=950cm=9.5m of fabric

LENGTH OF ONE CURTAIN
Choose the length of your curtains. Then add an extra 15cm for top and bottom turnings. With patterned fabric add the length of one pattern repeat also.

Sill-length curtains

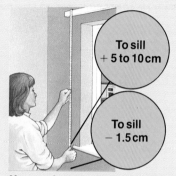

To sill + 5 to 10cm

To sill − 1.5cm

Measure from top of track to sill. Add 5 to 10cm. Or, if the sill protrudes, deduct 1.5cm.

Radiator-length curtains

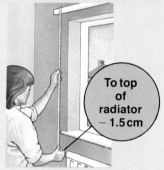

To top of radiator − 1.5cm

Measure from top of track to top of radiator. Deduct 1.5cm so the curtains will not touch the hot radiator.

Floor-length curtains

To floor − 1.5cm

Measure from top of track to floor. Deduct 1.5cm to stop the curtain from dragging and the hem from wearing.

NUMBER OF WIDTHS
Measure your curtain track and then look at the table below to work out how many widths of fabric are needed to cover it.

(This table also tells you how much heading tape you will need.)

If the track is very long get help with the measuring, especially if it is too high to reach from ground level.

How to use this table

1 Look along top line for the length of your track.

2 Look down left-hand column for your type of heading.

3 Find the point where the two meet. This shows the number of fabric widths you need and the length of tape.

NOTE Tape length given allows for turnings and matching pleats at centre edges of curtains.

Length of track (cm)		100	150	200	250	300	350	400	450	500
Standard heading (1½ × track length)	No. of 120cm widths	2	2	3	4	4	5	5	6	7
	Length of tape (cm)	260	260	380	500	500	620	620	740	860
Cluster (2 × track length)	No. of 120cm widths	2	3	4	5	6	6	7	8	9
	Length of tape (cm)	290	410	530	650	770	770	890	1010	1130
Decorative (2 × track length)	No. of 120cm widths	2	3	4	5	6	6	7	8	9
	Length of tape (cm)	260	380	500	620	740	740	860	980	1100
Triple pleats (2 × track length)	No. of 120cm widths	3	3	4	5	6	7	8	8	9
	Length of tape (cm)	410	410	530	650	770	890	1010	1010	1130
Cartridge pleats (2 × track length)	No. of 120cm widths	3	3	4	5	6	7	8	8	9
	Length of tape (cm)	410	410	530	650	770	890	1010	1010	1130
Pencil pleats (2½ × track length)	No. of 120cm widths	3	4	5	6	7	8	9	10	11
	Length of tape (cm)	380	500	620	740	860	980	1100	1220	1340
Box pleats (2½ × track length)	No. of 120cm widths	3	4	5	6	7	8	9	10	11
	Length of tape (cm)	410	530	650	770	890	1010	1130	1250	1370

Buying, preparing and cutting out fabric

Buying fabric

Curtains can be made in almost any natural or synthetic fabric. Your choice of fabric will depend on the style of the room and on your budget. Small prints and plain fabrics are easier on the pocket, as problems of matching designs during making up are minimal. Fabrics such as thick wools and tweeds will be heavy to stitch, while closely woven cotton is firm but easy to sew. A special fabric made of cotton sateen is sold for both detachable and integral linings.

Before you choose, buy 30cm or one pattern repeat, whichever is the greater. Arrange it over your window and check how it will look. It may be wise to do a shrink test before you start to make your curtains: fold the fabric in half widthways and cut two 10cm squares. If the fabric frays, zigzag stitch the edges. Wash and iron one square and compare it with the other. If the fabric shrinks, allow for a deeper hem.

Preparing the fabric

First straighten the raw edges along the grain of the fabric (the grain shows the direction of the weave). Along the length of the fabric these are the warp and widthways the weft threads.

Woven cottons or cotton mixtures: Using scissors, snip 2.5cm into selvedge at right-angles to the edge. Tear from snip to opposite edge.

Woven wools and linens: Snip 2.5cm into selvedge. Gently pull out a loose weft thread as shown here, and cut along the resulting line.

After straightening the cut edges, make sure the grain is also straight by pulling on the bias until the fabric is smooth and flat and all the corners form right-angles when the fabric is folded in half lengthways, selvedge to selvedge.

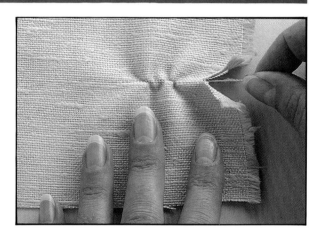

Finally, press the fabric to remove all creases. Before cutting out, mark the bottom of the fabric.

Cutting out fabric

To mark a right-angled cutting line, use a wooden metre ruler and a square-cornered object against the selvedge, then cut out.

Plain fabric

NOTE Cut plain fabric on the lengthways or widthways grain.

1 Measure the first length, keeping the rule in line with the selvedge. Mark the cutting line or pull a thread. Cut along the marked line.

2 Cut subsequent lengths as 1.

3 If you need any half widths to make up the curtains, fold one length in half lenghways, pinning selvedge to selvedge. Cut along fold. Half widths should be attached to outer edges.

Patterned fabric

NOTE Cut on the grain, but if large pattern does not follow the grain, cut to the pattern.

1 Mark bottom of pattern with tailor's chalk.

2 Make sure that, after allowing for hem turnings, the bottom of the pattern will lie on the hem edge. Trim off surplus fabric.

3 Cut out the fabrics as in 1, plain fabric, if necessary following the pattern.

4 Reposition the uncut fabric next to the

previous lengths which you have cut so that the two match exactly.

5 Repeat Step 4 to cut all lengths.

6 Cut and join half widths as for plain fabric, matching patterns.

How to make unlined curtains

WHAT YOU NEED

1 Curtain fabric
2 Curtain heading tape
3 Curtain hooks
Plus: Cutting-out and sewing scissors, tape measure, pins, needles, matching thread
Note When using track with hooks included, do not buy extra, separate hooks.

HOW TO WORK OUT YOUR QUANTITIES
Choose the shape and size of your curtain. Put up your track and decide on the heading (see page 7), then work out how much fabric you need (see page 8).

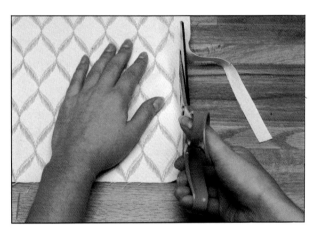

1 Prepare fabric and cut out (page 9). Cut the selvedge edge away from each side of each fabric width; discard. A tightly woven selvedge causes the seams to pucker.

2a **On plain fabrics:** Begin by placing two lengths with right sides together, matching raw edges. Pin and tack down one long edge, taking 1.5cm seam allowance

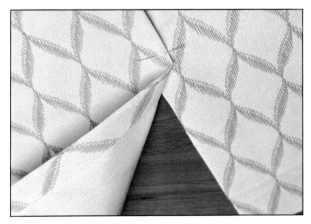

2b **On patterned fabrics:** The pattern must be matched exactly before stitching. Working from the right side of the fabric, tack the widths together using ladder stitch (page 12)

3 Once tacked, the fabric widths can be stitched together, using matching thread and flat fell seams (as shown on page 12) to form the complete curtain width

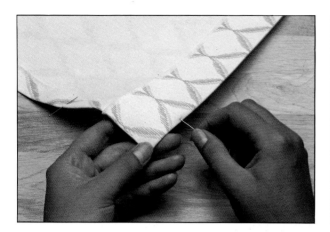

4 Turn in the side edges for 2cm and press. Turn up the hem edge for 5cm and press. Mark one hem width above hem. Measure one side hem width in from side edge; mark at hem

5 Fold in the corner at an uneven angle, folding from the marking pin at the side edge to the marking pin in the hem edge over the single side and base hems. Press the corner

6 Turn in the side seam again to form a double 2cm hem and press. Turn up the hem edge again, to form a double 5cm hem and press. Pin and tack side and hem edges

7 Finish the side and base hems: using matching thread, neatly slipstitch the side edges and hem edge, taking care that stitching does not show on right side (see page 12)

8 Place the fabric flat and measure the length up from the hem edge. Press excess at top to wrong side and trim. Position curtain tape close to folded edge. Pin and tack

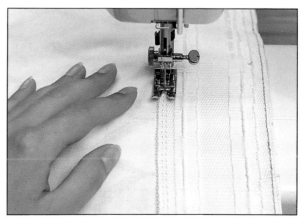

9 Stitch tape in place following the marked lines. Pull up tape to the correct width from the outside edge of curtain. Knot cords together, do not cut. Hang curtains

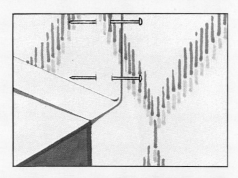

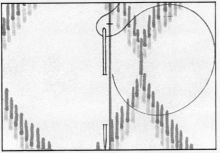

Ladder stitch

Ladder stitch is the professional way to tack two pieces of patterned fabric together so that the design will match perfectly across the seamline.

1 Press under 1.5cm seam allowance down first length of fabric. Place this folded edge over the 1.5cm seam allowance on the second fabric length. Pin in place
2 Work from the right side of the fabric with a single thread. Take the thread into and along the fold of the seam allowance, bringing it out about 1.5cm further along the fold
3 Take thread across to the flat fabric and run needle along the seamline; bringing it out about 1.5cm along the seamline. Continue working across join with small straight stitches. The fabric can now be folded with right sides together, and seam stitched

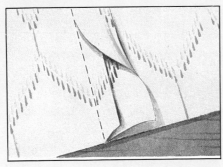

Flat fell seam

This seam is especially useful for unlined home furnishings where the seam must be hard-wearing.

1 Place the two fabrics with right sides together, raw edges matching. Pin, tack and stitch together 1.5cm from raw edges. Trim one seam allowance to 5mm. Leave remaining allowance
2 Fold the wider complete seam allowance evenly in half, raw edge to seamline, at the same time enclosing narrower 5mm seam allowance inside the folded allowance.
3 Press the folded edge over again so that it lies flat against main fabric and the narrow seam allowance is entirely hidden. Pin and tack down complete length of the seam
4 Working from the wrong side of the fabric, stitch along the seam again, positioning stitching along the folded edge. This will enclose all raw edges and provide a neat finish

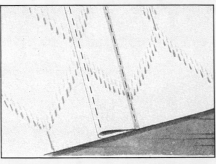

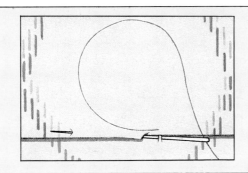

Slipstitch hem

This is the most common form of hem and is almost invisible on the right side.

1 Fasten a length of thread in the hem. Bring the needle out of the fold of the hem. Pick up one/two threads of flat fabric directly below the hem
2 Take the needle back into the fold and run it through for about 2cm. Continue as above

How to make a detachable lining

WHAT YOU NEED
1 Curtain lining fabric
2 Lining heading tape
Plus: Cutting-out and small scissors, tape, pins, needles, tacking and matching thread
To catch the detachable lining to the curtains you will need either:
Poppers and 5mm-wide tape *or* 1cm-wide tape, *or* tape and touch-and-close fastening

HOW TO WORK OUT YOUR QUANTITIES
Work out the amount of fabric you need in the same way as for curtains, following the instructions on page 8. However, bear in mind that the lining must be 2.5cm shorter than the curtain so that it will not be visible when the curtain is hung. Detachable linings should be one and a half to two times the track length, so follow amounts for standard tape on page 8.

Make the linings following steps 1 to 7 on pages 10 and 11, then continue as below

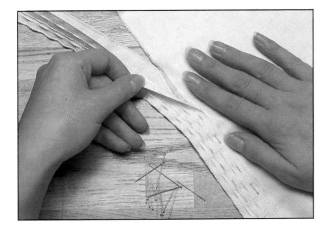

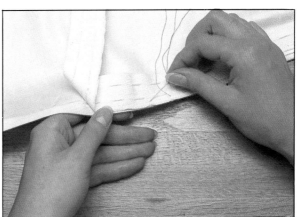

1a **If you are using pocketed lining tape,** measure from lining hem up and position top of lining between the two sides of lining tape. Pin, tack and stitch tape in place

1b **If you are using a flat lining tape,** turn 6mm to wrong side and press. Place lining tape over top hem, flush with folded top edge. Pin, tack and stitch tape in place

Hold detachable lining in place with one of the following along any seams and inside the side edges at about 30cm intervals

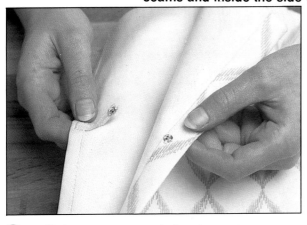

2a **Using poppers,** stitch a 2.5cm length of 5mm-wide tape to the lining. Stitch a popper top to the free end of the tape. Stitch the opposite half of the popper to the curtain *or*

2b **Using 1cm-wide tape,** stitch a 15cm length to both lining and curtain. Tie in a loose bow. Or, stitch a length of touch-and-close fastening to tape and curtain

How to make attached linings

WHAT YOU NEED

1 Curtain fabric
2 Lining fabric
3 Curtain weights
4 Curtain heading tape
5 Curtain hooks
Plus: Cutting-out and small scissors, tape measure or rule, pins, needles, tacking thread and matching thread, tailor's chalk

NOTE: Check your curtain track before you buy curtain hooks, as some rails come complete with integral hooks.

HOW TO WORK OUT YOUR QUANTITIES

Fix curtain pole or track in position at the window. Measure up for lined curtains as for unlined curtains (see page 8). To work out how much lining you need, measure up as for unlined curtains and deduct 10cm per fabric width. Remember when making linings that you will not need extra fabric for matching the pattern. If the curtains are to hang from a pole, measure from the base of the pole, then choose a heading tape that can be hung below the pole, so that the latter becomes a feature. (For heading tapes see page 7.)

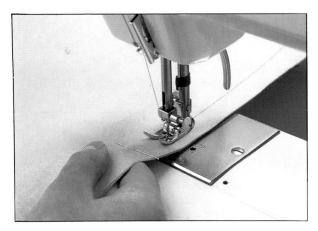

1 Cut out fabrics as on page 9, making each lining drop 10cm shorter. Stitch widths together with flat seams taking 1.5cm seam allowance. Repeat to stitch lining width

2 Turn in 6.5cm down each side of curtain fabric and press. Turn up 15cm hem and press. Unfold. Mitre bottom corners as Steps 4-6, page 11, taking only single turnings

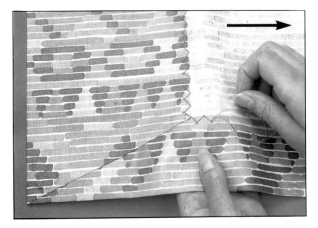

3 Add single weights or a length of weights inside the hem, as shown opposite. Slipstitch across the mitres at each corner. Herringbone stitch down the sides and along bottom hems

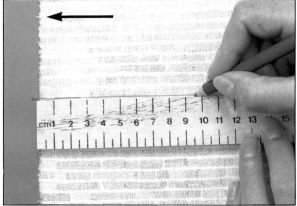

4 Lay curtain flat, right side down, and mark down centre with pins; draw centre line using tailor's chalk. Starting at centre, mark chalk lines, 30cm apart, to both side edges

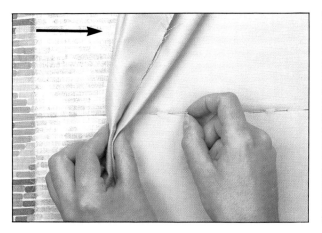

5 With wrong sides facing, centre lining over main curtain with raw edge of lining level with curtain, top and bottom. Pin fabric and lining together along centre line

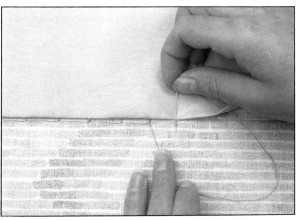

6 Using thread to match curtain fabric, lockstitch fabrics together carefully. Begin at top edge and end just above curtain hem. Repeat down each chalk line

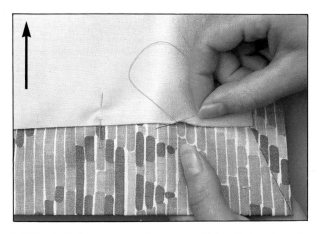

7 Tack lining to curtain at top. Trim lining level with curtain at sides. Turn in lining side edges by 2cm and hem by 5cm. Press. Slipstitch lining to curtain along sides and hem

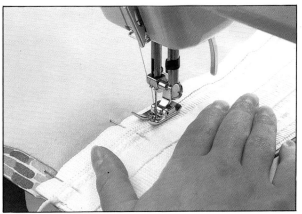

8 Turn in both top edges by 2cm. Press. Position heading tape to curtain top; stitch in place through all thicknesses. Pull up cords evenly and knot them together

How to add curtain weights inside the hem

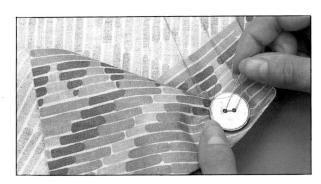

3a **If using circular weights,** position them inside each mitre. Using thread to match curtain, stitch to hem as if sewing on a button. Repeat inside hem at each seam, *or*

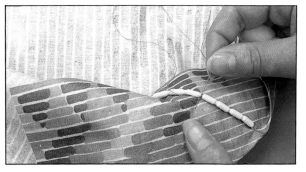

3b **If using fabric-encased weights,** cut to hem length. Lay the weights inside the curtain hem, along pressed hem line. Using matching thread, stitch to hem at intervals

How to make loose linings

WHAT YOU NEED

1 Curtain fabric
2 Lining fabric
3 Curtain weights
4 Curtain heading tape
5 Curtain hooks

Plus: Large cutting-out and small sewing scissors; tape measure, pins, needles, tacking and matching thread

HOW TO WORK OUT YOUR QUANTITIES

Measure up as for unlined curtains (see page 8). On long curtains deduct 1.5cm from length so hem will not drag on the floor. Lining should be same width, but 10cm shorter.

Loose-lined curtains hanging at doors

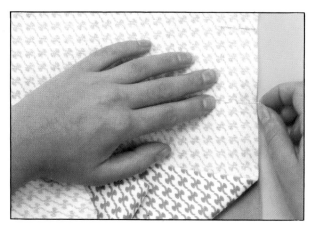

1 Make up curtains and lining, making lining 8cm shorter and 4cm narrower. Mark centres. Match curtain and lining, right sides together, match sides and top

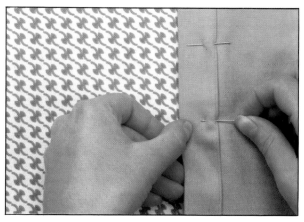

2 Using plain flat seams, stitch the side edges to within 18cm of bottom edge with 1.5cm seam allowance. Turn up a double 2.5cm hem on lining. Pin, tack and stitch

3 Turn up a 2.5cm hem on curtain. Press in mitre corner; turn up a further 2.5cm. Turn in sides for 3.5cm. Slipstitch. Turn to right side. Match centres, press to form 2cm margins

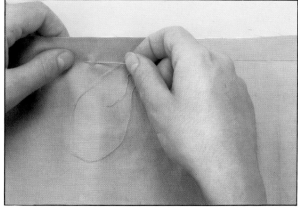

4 Slipstitch remaining lining edges at each side to side edges of curtains. Tack curtain and lining together along top edge. Following Steps 7–9, page 11, stitch on heading tape

Decorative nets

Choose from a wide range of sheer fabrics to make nets that will transform any window into a striking feature from inside and out.

Fine net curtains can be decorative as well as practical, being delicate enough to let the light flood in.

Sheer fabrics are sold in a huge range of natural and synthetic fibres, or as a blend.

Nets are hung from covered wire, fine rod or adjustable poles, all slotted through a casing hem. But you can also use a lightweight track designed for use with heading tape and hang the nets like conventional curtains.

How to make cross-over net curtains

WHAT YOU NEED
Sheer curtain fabric
Plus: tacking thread and thread to match fabric, fine needles, lace pins, tape measure, large cutting-out and small sewing scissors, tailor's chalk.

NOTE The curtain shown on page 17 is threaded on to a decorative brass rod fitted outside the area of the window. However, it could also be hung inside the architrave on a wire specially designed for nets. Hang the wire on small hooks screwed to the window frame.

HOW TO WORK OUT YOUR QUANTITIES
Measure your window as for curtains, see page 8. Allow two or two-and-a-half times the window width—depending on fullness required—if nets are to be hung on wire or poles. Allow 5cm for a double casing hem at the top. When using heading tape and track, add the top allowance as for curtains page 8. When a frill is added, deduct the frill depth from curtain length. For the frill, measure both sides and hem edge and allow twice this measurement for each curtain by the depth of the frill, plus seam allowances and hem.

1 Make two curtains in the same way. Cut sufficient fabric widths to the required size (page 8). Matching the patterns using ladder stitch, join widths with flat fell seams (page 12)

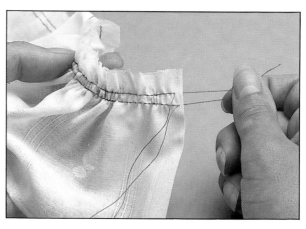

2 Make an 8cm-wide frill (Steps 3 to 4 on page 21). Measure both side edges and bottom edge of curtain and make up frill strips to twice this length. Gather top edge of frill

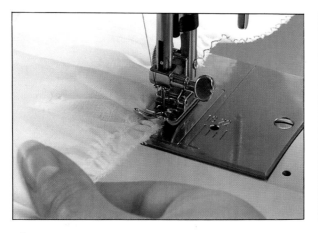

3 With right sides together, pin, tack and stitch frill to each curtain along sides and base edges. Trim down seam allowance. Zigzag raw edges together to neaten or overcast by hand

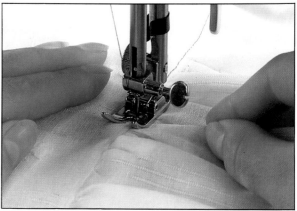

4 To ensure that the frill hangs well, press neatened seam allowance in towards curtain. On the right side edge-stitch on the curtain alongside seam through all layers

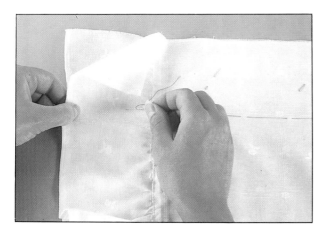

5 With right sides uppermost, position the two curtains one on top of the other, matching top edges. Pin and tack together across the top of the curtains 8cm from top raw edges

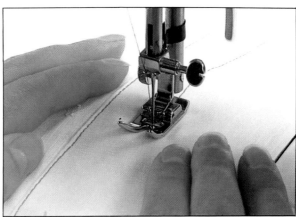

6 To form casing and frill turn under top edges along tacked line. Turn under raw edges again for 1cm; pin, tack and stitch hem. Stitch again 3cm above previous stitching to form a casing

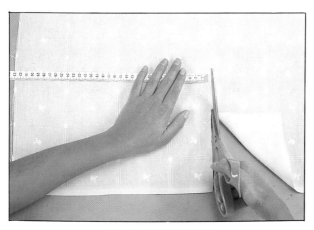

7 After hanging the curtains, gather up each curtain separately and measure round for tie-backs, adding 150cm for the bows. Make up two fabric pieces to this length by 33cm width

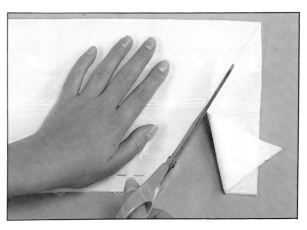

8 Make up two tie-backs: fold fabric in half lengthways, right sides together, matching edges. Mark 11cm from each end on raw edges. Cut from mark to fold to form diagonal end

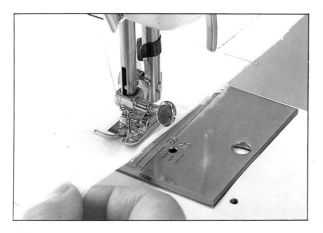

9 Taking 1.5cm seam allowance, stitch all round raw edges of folded tie-backs, leaving an opening in the centre of straight edge. Trim to 5mm. Turn to right side

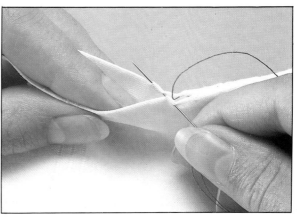

10 Turn in opening edges, and slipstitch to close. Tie round each curtain and into a bow. Stitch a curtain ring to it, and hang on a hook fixed to architrave

How to make a jardiniere net curtain

WHAT YOU NEED

1 Sheer curtain fabric
2 Ribbon to cover frill seam
Plus: Cutting-out and small sewing scissors, tacking and matching thread, tape measure, lace pins, fine needles, dressmaker's pattern paper or brown paper for pattern.

NOTE: This net curtain (shown on page 2) is hung on a covered wire, but it could also be hung on a thin pole. Both should be fixed inside the architrave. Follow instructions for preparing the fabric on page 9.

HOW TO WORK OUT YOUR QUANTITIES

Fix up the curtain wire inside the window architrave. Measure from the wire to the window sill; this will be the finished measurement. The frill is 15cm wide, so deduct this from the curtain length and add 5cm for top casing hem and 1.5cm for seam allowance. Allow for two to two-and-a-half times the width of the curtain wire. For the frill, allow for twice the curtain width by 18cm. Take into account the fabric width and when working out your quantities try to arrange the seams in the best position for the window.

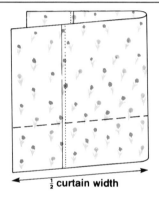

½ curtain width

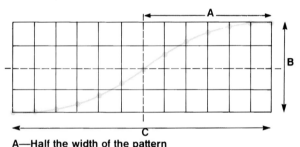

A—**Half the width of the pattern**
B—**The height of the pattern**
C—**Half the width of the curtain**

HOW TO CUT OUT YOUR PATTERN

Fold curtain in half and measure the width. Cut a piece of brown paper to this width by one third of the curtain length. Divide this paper in half both lengthways and widthways to find middle point (where dotted lines cross). Divide up paper into equal areas. Plot the bottom line of your curtain across pattern. Cut out.

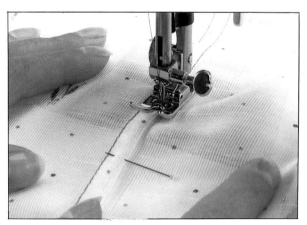

1 Cut out, pin, tack and stitch widths together using flat fell seams (page 12). Fold curtains in half lengthways with right sides together, matching side edges and seams. Pin together

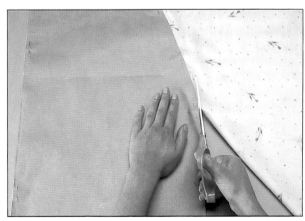

2 Make a paper pattern for the curved bottom edge as shown above. Pin pattern to bottom edge of curtain and carefully cut out along the curved line. Unfold curtain

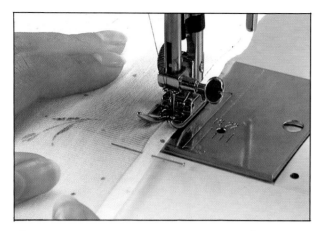

3 Stitch frill into one length with flat fell seams. Turn under 5mm and then turn under 5mm again to form a double hem along bottom edge of frill. Pin, tack and stitch hem

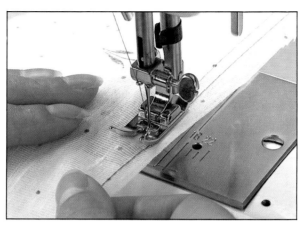

4 Work two rows of gathering stitches along top edge of frill, the first row 1cm from raw edge, the second row just under 1.5cm from raw edge. Pull up the gathers evenly

5 With wrong sides together, pin frill to bottom edge of curtain, pulling up frill gathers evenly to fit curtain edge. Pin, tack and stitch together, taking 1.5cm seam allowance

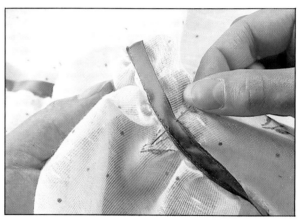

6 Trim down seam allowance to 5mm and press up towards curtain. Position ribbon over seam, covering raw edges. Pin, tack and stitch ribbon along both edges

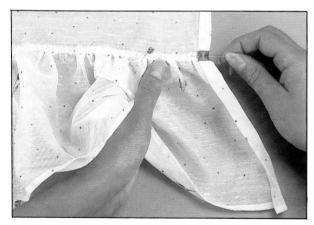

7 Turn under 1cm along both side edges, including raw side edges of frill and ribbon. Turn under 1cm again to form a double 1cm hem. Pin, tack and stitch side hems in place

8 Turn under 2.5cm along top edge of curtain. Turn under 2.5cm again to form a double 2.5cm casing hem. Pin, tack and stitch hem casing in place. Thread with wire and hang

Curtain tie-backs

Smarten up your curtains with stylish tie-backs—easily made from the minimum of fabric

Tie-backs give curtains a finished look. They are made from two layers of fabric with stiffening in between. Curtain rings sewn to the ends are used to attach each tie-back to a hook on the wall. They can be made up in a variety of shapes to suit your personal taste, but the plain, straight tie-back will go with almost any type of curtain design. You can choose a matching or contrasting fabric for the tie-backs, and, if fabric is short or rather heavy, use a toning lining for the wrong side. Leave the tie-backs plain and simple or add a decorative trim.

How to make a straight tie-back

WHAT YOU NEED
1 Fabric
2 Heavy-weight interfacing
3 Curtain rings
Plus: Scissors, matching and tacking thread, pins, needles

HOW TO WORK OUT YOUR QUANTITIES
Make a paper pattern and cut one piece from scrap fabric. Check this round your curtain for length and width. Then use to work out fabric requirements.

1 Cut out one piece of interfacing, two of fabric. Pin interfacing centrally to wrong side of one fabric piece

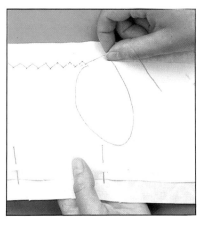

2 Herringbone stitch the interfacing to the fabric as shown, picking up only one fabric thread with each stitch

3 Right sides together, stitch second fabric piece to interfaced fabric, leaving an 8cm side opening. Trim

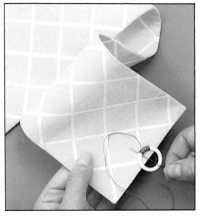

4 Turn to right side. Turn in opening edges; slipstitch. Blanket stitch a curtain ring to each end as shown

Frilled tie-back
To add a 3cm-wide frill, measure round outer edge and cut a bias strip twice this measurement, and 9cm wide. Fold in half lengthways and gather raw edges together. Pin and stitch frill round interfaced tie-back, along stitching line. Complete Steps 3 and 4.

Piped tie-back
Add contrasting piping to all edges of tie-back. Make up piping (pages 64-5) to required length; stitch in place around interfaced tie-back. Complete Steps 3 and 4.

Straight tie-back

Frilled tie-back

Piped tie-back

Roller blinds

One of the most practical and economical window treatments—
especially for small windows—is the roller blind. An attractive blind
can easily be run up in a few hours

Blinds take much less fabric than curtains and are particularly suitable in kitchens and bathrooms where curtains can get in the way. However, they can be used in any room in the house.

Roller blinds are very easy to make, simply consisting of flat, stiffened fabric fixed to a wooden roller and hung from special brackets, secured at each side of the window frame. A spring mechanism in one end of the roller acts as a pulley so that the blind can be raised completely to let in the maximum amount of light during the day and to give privacy when they are lowered at night.

Roller blinds are most successful on narrow to medium width windows. On very wide ones, the blinds can easily lose their flush, flat appearance and go out of shape. If you must cover a wide window, use two or three blinds positioned so that their edges are over the window struts. They also make excellent coverings for shelves, wardrobes or cupboards in confined spaces because they don't open out into the room as doors do (see page 29).

The lower edge of the blind can be finished in a variety of ways, as described on page 30. Plain blinds can also be decorated with braid or cord in the same way as curtains.

Choosing fabric

Firm, closely-woven fabric is best. If the fabric is too light or loosely-woven, it tends to stretch and the blind will have wavy edges; also it will not cut out light satisfactorily. If the fabric is too heavy it will roll up unevenly and be too thick around the roller.

Pre-stiffened blind fabrics are the easiest option. They come in wide widths and in a good choice of colours and patterns. They have a spongeable, fade-resistant finish and do not fray at the edges.

However, if you wish to use an ordinary cotton furnishing fabric to match up the blind fabric with the decor of the room, you will have to use one of the various blind stiffening products on the market. Because PVC is waterproof, it is an ideal choice for bathrooms and kitchens and the side edges can be stuck rather than sewn. It is important to have side hems or the edges will not lie flat. Stiffening products also allow you to use a lace roller blind as an alternative to the more conventional net curtains.

Try to make the blind from one fabric width. If you must join two, split the second down the middle and stitch one half either side of the central panel with flat fell seams.

Roller blind kits

The basic hardware needed to make roller blinds can be bought in the form of a kit. This consists of a wooden roller which has a detachable cap and pin at one end and a spring winding mechanism at the other. Also included in the kit are brackets to fit either into a recessed window or at each side of an ordinary window. In addition, there is a batten or lath to be inserted at the base of the blind to weight it so that it hangs well. There is also a cord holder and a cord. Heavy-duty kits can be bought for large windows. If you cannot buy a kit of the exact length you need, buy the size up and cut the roller.

Fabric stiffeners

All fabrics, other than special blind fabrics, need to be stiffened in order to make a successful roller blind. This treatment will make them less likely to fray and mean that they will roll without crinkling at the edges. Certain stiffening products are available in the form of aerosol or liquid sprays. Most fabrics will shrink slightly when treated with either form so allow for this.

Alternatively, for small blinds, you can use an iron-on woven interfacing. This is ironed to the wrong side of the blind fabric after the side hems have been formed.

How to measure for roller blinds

Where you position your roller blind is purely a matter of personal taste. However, where there is a deep recess it is usual to position the blind against the glazed area of the window. In the case of windows where there is no recess, the blind has to be flat-mounted on the wall or window frame. In this case, it will depend on the window surround as to where the brackets are fixed.

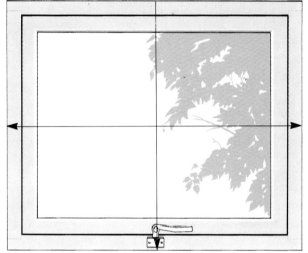

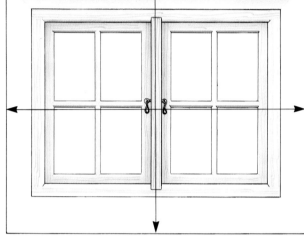

On a window without a recess, where the blind is wall-mounted, more light will be excluded if the blind extends beyond the top and sides of the window. How much extra allowance you need will depend on the window frame. Unless there is a flat piece that will support a bracket, the blind will have to be mounted beyond the frame. Decide on the size of roller kit to buy by marking the positions of the brackets on either side of the window (right).

On a recessed window, use a metal ruler to measure horizontally from one side of the recess to the other in a straight line. Deduct 1.5cm at each edge to leave enough room on the right for the pin end and on the left for the spring mechanisms. If you cannot buy a roller kit of exactly this length, buy the next size up and cut down the roller after fitting the brackets. Position the brackets 3cm from the top of the recess to allow for the full roller.

How to make a roller blind from a kit

WHAT YOU NEED
1 Blind kit, the correct length or longer
2 Fabric
3 Stiffening product
Plus: Cutting-out and small sewing scissors, metre stick or metal rule, pins, needles, tacking and matching thread.

NOTE Because roller blinds are flat against the window it is a good opportunity to use a picture fabric. In this case, as well as centring the main parts of the fabric, choose a good position for the base edge of the blind as the elephant's feet and lion's head were positioned on the blind on page 24. Allow for hem casing below this point.

HOW TO WORK OUT YOUR QUANTITIES
First find your roller size by measuring the width of your window accurately with a metre stick or retractable metal rule (see above). Fix the brackets into position. Either fit the roller in place or trim to fit and then slot into the brackets. For the fabric length measure from the fixed roller to the desired base level using a retractable metal rule. Add 26cm to this measurement for bottom hem casing and top hem, and to ensure that when extended the roller will still be covered by fabric.

For the fabric width, measure the length of the wooden part of the roller and add 2cm to this measurement to allow for side hems. On a large print allow for centring the design.

1 Mark, then fix brackets at the top of window, with round pinhole bracket on right-hand side. Fit square end of mechanism in its bracket. Check roller length and trim if necessary

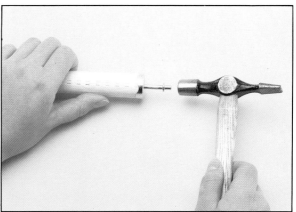

2 Place cap over cut end of roller. Hold roller horizontally on a table, fit pin into hole and gently hammer into place. Place roller in brackets to check fit

3 Square off fabric before cutting out by drawing one thread across the fabric width and using the line as a cutting guide. Cut off both selvedge edges. Cut a piece of fabric to the required size

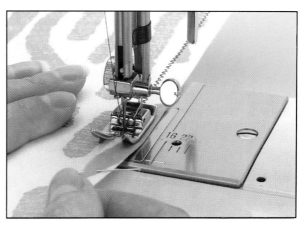

4 At each side edge, turn a 1cm-wide hem to the wrong side. Pin, tack and press hems in place. Zigzag stitch down both side edges with the raw edges centred under the zigzags

5 At the base of the blind, turn up 1cm then 4cm to form the bottom casing. Pin, tack and stitch along the casing, close to the top of the hem fold and across one end of casing

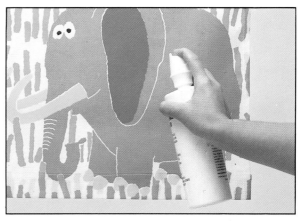

6 Before stiffening the fabric, iron well to remove creases. Spray in a well ventilated area, allow to dry and repeat if necessary. Dry following manufacturer's instructions

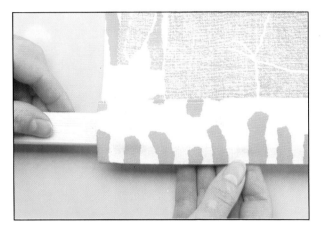

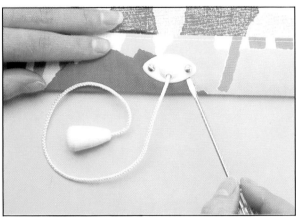

7 Trim wooden lath to 1.5cm shorter than blind width. Insert lath into the casing. Stitch side opening by hand to close the casing and hold the lath firmly in position

8 Make up cord pull by threading one end of the cord through cord holder; knot. Thread opposite end through acorn; knot. Screw down holder at centre of lath casing, on wrong side

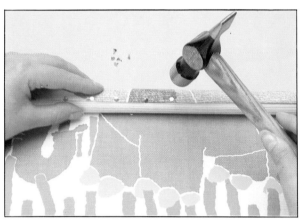

9 If the roller does not have a guideline marked, draw a line along its length with a pencil and long rule. Press 1.5cm hem to the right side along top edge of blind

10 With blind fabric right side up, lay roller across the blind with the spring mechanism on left. Place top folded edge along marked line. Tack in place at 2cm intervals

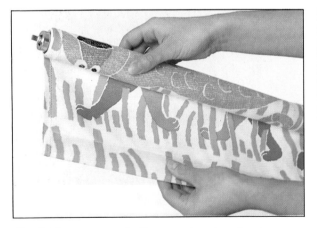

11 To ensure winding mechanism is at correct tension, roll up blind by hand and insert into brackets with fabric against window. Pull blind down to cover window

12 If necessary, repeat Step 11—remove blind from brackets, roll up by hand and replace in the brackets—several times in order to get the tension of the spring correct

How to make a blind from stiffened fabric

WHAT YOU NEED

1 Blind kit, as before
2 Specially stiffened fabric
3 Adhesive tape
Plus: Cutting-out and small sewing scissors, set square and metre stick, matching thread, needles

NOTE Stiffened fabric is sold in wide widths so, when using a plain fabric, check if you can cut the blind length from the fabric width. (This could save quite a lot of fabric.) It does not join together well.

HOW TO WORK OUT YOUR QUANTITIES

Measure up window for the roller blind size as for fabric blind (see page 26), following the instructions for the type of window you want to cover. Measure the roller for fabric in the same way as for fabric blind (see page 26), but omit allowance for side hems. Only add 25cm to the length measurement for top and base hems. Even though there is no need to have a double hem at the top edge, a double thickness of fabric will provide firm anchorage for the fixing tacks and prevent the fabric from splitting.

Plain stiffened fabric blinds smartly cover twin alcoves. The blind decorations are positioned at different points on the fabric so that if the left-hand blind is only half-drawn for display purposes, the decorations can align.

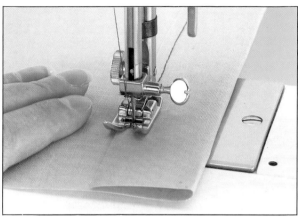

1 Fix brackets to window and trim roller to correct size as Steps 1 and 2, page 27. Then, using a set square to achieve a straight edge, cut the fabric to the required size

2 At the base, turn up a single 4cm hem to the wrong side. Hold in place with short strips of adhesive tape. Stitch along hem and one side. Insert lath and close opening as Step 7, page 28

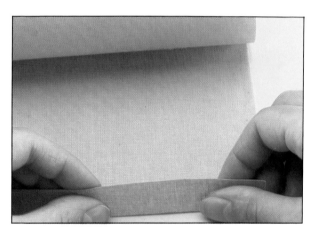

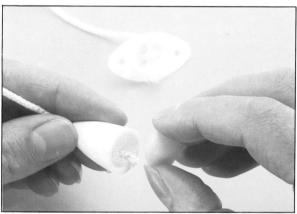

3 At top edge, turn down a 1.5cm hem to the right side. Press along fold firmly with your fingers to hold hem in place. Tack to roller as Step 10, page 28

4 Make up and attach cord pull with the acorn and fix to wrong side of lath casing, Step 8, page 28. Slot into brackets, tension spring mechanism as Steps 11 and 12, page 28

Decorative edges

A decorative edge will improve the look of a roller blind. How the edge is made depends on the fabric used.

PVC and the stiffened fabric sold for blinds can be cut to form a decorative shaped edge without facing or neatening.

When using cotton furnishing fabric, the edge must be faced. The facing can either be cut without seam allowance to the exact shape of the decorative edge and zigzagged to neaten blind, or both facing and edge may be cut with 1cm seam allowance, stitched and turned.

For first method, turn in 1cm on top and side edges of facing, then position to blind with wrong sides together, matching edges. Stitch one side and across blind, close to fold and again 4cm below to form lath casing. Finish casing as for Steps 7 and 8, page 28. Neaten edges by close zigzagging together in a contrasting colour.

For second method cut out edge and facing with seam allowance. Turn 1cm to wrong side along top edge of facing and stitch. Right sides together, stitch facing to blind, along base and side edges. Finish side edges of blind as Step 4, page 27. Trim and turn.

Austrian blinds

Give your windows a completely new look with Austrian blinds.
They are very simple to make, yet their soft gathers add a touch
of extravagant luxury to both modern and traditional rooms

ustrian blinds are based on the same principle as festoon and roman blinds in that they are drawn up by cords that are threaded through a fine heading tape stitched in vertical rows to the back of the blind. However, these blinds are softer in appearance since they are also gathered across the top on pencil-pleated heading tape to produce extravagant ruffles of fabric. The soft swags are emphasized with a base-edge frill, while a plain or gathered border can be added at the side edges. Austrian blinds are best left unlined so that they can easily be drawn up in soft gathers. Because of this, you will achieve the best results if you choose a cotton or cotton-mix fabric that looks good with the light behind it.

How to measure your window

Austrian blinds hang at the window on curtain track fixed to the front of a length of 50mm by 25mm battening. On a recessed window (see page 26), where the battening is fixed into the ceiling of the recess, measure from one side of the recess to the other to find the length of battening. On a window without a recess (see right), the battening should be fitted above the window. It should extend 15cm beyond the edges of a plain window and should be flush with the edges of a moulded architrave. On all windows, the track is the same length as the battening, and the depth should be measured from the track to the sill.

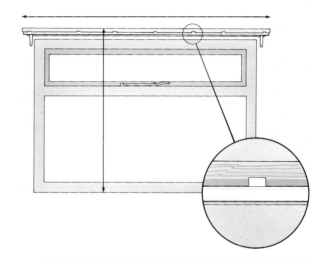

How to make a frilled Austrian blind

WHAT YOU NEED

1 Fabric
2 1.5cm-wide lightweight narrow heading tape
3 7.5cm-wide pencil-pleated heading tape
4 Nylon cord
5 1.5cm-diameter curtain rings
6 50mm × 25mm battening and fixing screws
7 Standard curtain track and runners hooks
8 Screw eyes
9 Primer, undercoat and gloss paint
10 Cleat and fixing screws
Plus: Sewing equipment, drill, bit, screwdriver, bradawl, paintbrush, glasspaper

HOW TO WORK OUT YOUR QUANTITIES

For the fabric length, measure from the battening to the sill and add one third again. For the width, double the battening length. For the frill, allow for 14cm depth by twice the blind width. For the vertical tapes, measure blind width and allow for them to be 30cm apart. Curtain rings are threaded into the tapes at 20cm intervals. For top heading tape, measure the blind width. For each length of cord, double the finished blind length and add the width measurement. Multiply by the number of vertical tapes.

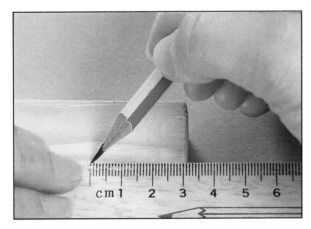

1 Cut the battening to fit the window. Mark and drill the fixing holes to the underside (50mm-wide side) of battening, positioning first holes 3cm from both ends

2 Drill the remaining holes about 40cm apart, between the two outer holes. Paint the battening to match the window, using primer, undercoat and then gloss paint

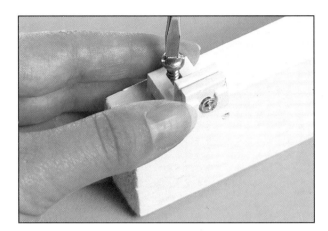

3 Cut and fix a length of curtain track to fit the front edge of battening. Fix with end-stops in place, threading on to the track sufficient runners for the blind

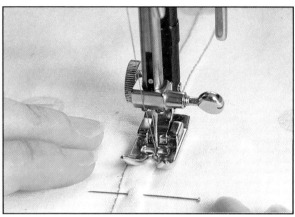

4 Cut out fabric for blind. If necessary, pin, tack and stitch widths together with flat fell seams (page 12) to gain the correct blind width matching design as shown on page 12

5 Turn in both side edges of blind for 1cm and then again for a further 1cm to form a double hem. Pin, tack and stitch both side hems in place

6 For frill, cut out 14cm-wide strips of fabric which, when stitched together, will be twice the base edge length. Stitch frill lengths together with French seams (page 41)

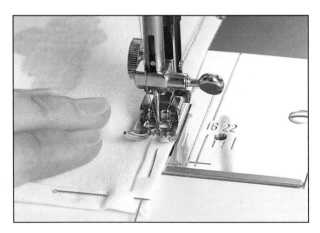

7 Turn under base and side edges of frill to make a double 1cm hem with mitred corners. Stitch hems in place. Run two rows of gathering stitches along top raw edges

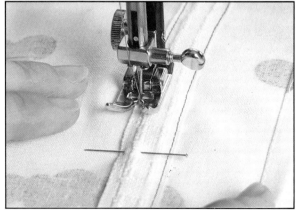

8 On the wrong side of the blind, mark positions of outer rows of vertical heading tapes, 4cm from hemmed edges. Pin, tack and stitch tapes in place

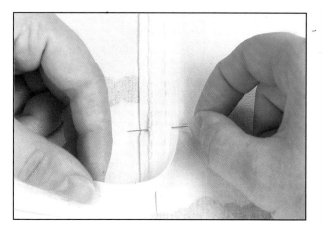

9 Measure between the two outer rows of tape and divide distance equally to find the positions of the remaining rows, about 30cm apart. Stitch tapes into position

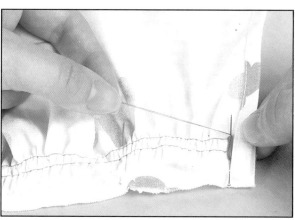

10 Position frill to base edge, matching side hem edges and pulling up gathering threads. Pin, tack and stitch, taking 2cm seam allowance on raw edge of blind

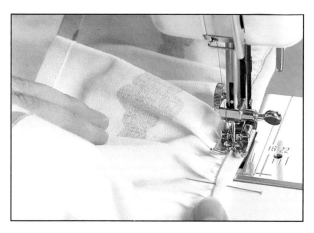

11 Trim frill turnings. Turn under raw edge of blind seam allowance and fold flat against the blind, catching in raw ends of tapes and frill turnings. Stitch

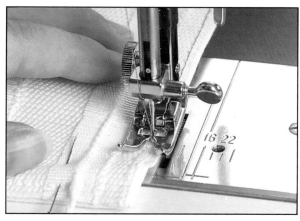

12 Turn down top edge of blind for 1.5cm. With wrong sides together, position heading to blind 6mm from top. Turn under side edges, leaving cords free at one end. Stitch

13 Thread curtain rings through vertical tapes, positioning first row of rings 2cm from frill seam and last row 15cm from top. Space other rings in between about 20cm apart

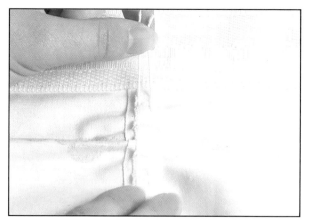

14 Pull up each vertical tape in turn, making sure that the gathers match. Wind excess cord into loops and tie into bows, to hold them in position at the top of each row

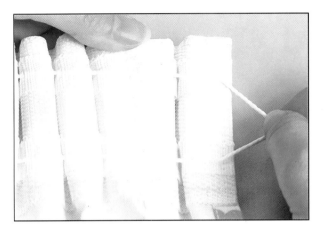

15 Pull up top heading tape till blind measures the width of the curtain track. Wind excess cords together at one side and knot to hold together as Step 14

16 Fix screw eyes to the underside of the battening, positioning the first two 5cm in from ends. Fix more screw eyes in between matching rows of vertical tape

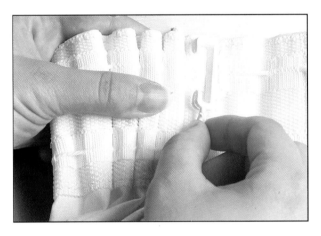

17 Thread curtain hooks through top heading tape and then on to the track, spacing them about 10cm apart and fixing the outer edges on to the end-stops to fix blind

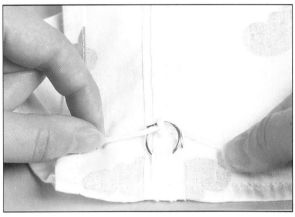

18 Cut cord as required and tie a length to first ring on bottom outer edge. Thread cord through all rings on the tape to the top. Repeat with each length of cord

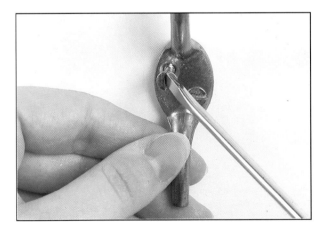

19 Fix the cleat beside the window, either to the wood surround or to the wall. Mark the position through the screw holes with a bradawl, then screw the cleat in place

20 Thread each cord in turn through screw eyes along the top of the battening till all cords hang together at one side. Knot cords together, trim and wind round cleat

BED LINEN

Throw-over bedspreads

The simplest way to cover a bed is with a throw-over bedspread—choose a striking patterned fabric that will give the bedroom a totally new look

In modern homes, bedrooms tend to be small, and the bedspread is a very important part of the decor. The easiest and perhaps the most effective bedspread is a simple throw-over cover. The easiest, as it is made from two lengths of fabric, and most effective, because the seamlines are disguised on the bed. Try to choose a crease-resistant, colour-fast fabric that will wear well. The bedspread fabric can match the wallpaper, curtains and even bedside tablecloths, but take care that the amount of pattern in the room is not overwhelming. Then decide on the design—if there is a valance on the bed, you could make a bedspread that falls short, exposing some of the valance. Once the length is chosen, you can pick rounded or straight base corners. You can also enhance a plain cover by adding a fringe or self frill.

How to make a lined bedspread

WHAT YOU NEED

1 Fabric
2 Lining fabric
Plus: Cutting-out and small sewing scissors, pins, needles, tape measure, matching and tacking threads
NOTE When choosing fabric, bear in mind that the bedspread will look much better with two seams on either side of the bed top rather than with a central seam. As the fabric area is large, you can use a large-print fabric to good effect, but allow extra fabric as matching the pattern will be important.

HOW TO WORK OUT YOUR QUANTITIES

Measure the bed with all the bedclothes in position. For the length, measure from the mattress over the pillows down to the foot end. Then measure the depth to the floor. Add 10cm to the length for hems. For the width, measure from side to side across the bed, then add twice the depth to floor measurement. Add 10cm to the width for hems. If you like extra fabric to tuck under the pillows, add an extra 50cm to the length. For lining fabric, repeat measurements, omitting any extra fabric allowed for pattern matching.

1 From fabric, cut out two lengths to the required size, matching pattern. Trim off selvedges from both sides of each length. Cut one piece of fabric in half lengthways.

2 Fold under seam allowance along edge of one half-width and place over seam allowance of centre piece, matching pattern. Ladder stitch (page 12) together from right side

3 Ladder stitch second half-width to opposite long edge of centre piece. Stitch with plain flat seams. Trim side widths to correct length plus 5cm hem allowance

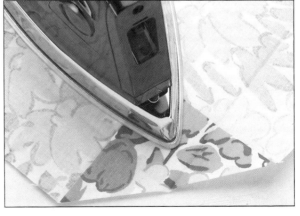

4 Press seams open. Turn under a 5cm single hem on all edges of bedspread and press. Mitre all corners: unfold pressed hem at first corner, press in diagonally across point

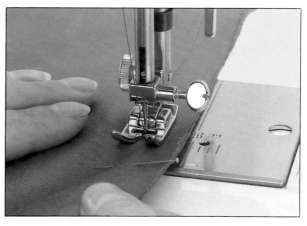

5 Refold hem. Repeat to form a mitre at each corner. Slipstitch folded edges together at each corner. Pin, tack and herringbone stitch all round the hem edge of bedspread as shown

6 From lining fabric, cut out two pieces the same length as fabric. Trim centre width then pin, tack and stitch together with plain flat seams, taking 1.5cm seam allowances

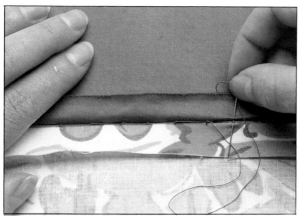

7 Position lining over fabric with wrong sides facing. Pin together down both seams. Fold back lining at each side to pin line. Lockstitch lining to fabric along outer seam allowances

8 Trim outer edge of lining level with hem edge of bedspread. Turn under a 3cm single hem on all edges, mitring corners to match. Pin, tack and slipstitch lining fabric round outer edge

Duvet covers

Now that extra-wide sheeting fabric is readily available, making your own duvet covers has become a very simple, money-saving proposition and a good way to co-ordinate bedroom furnishings

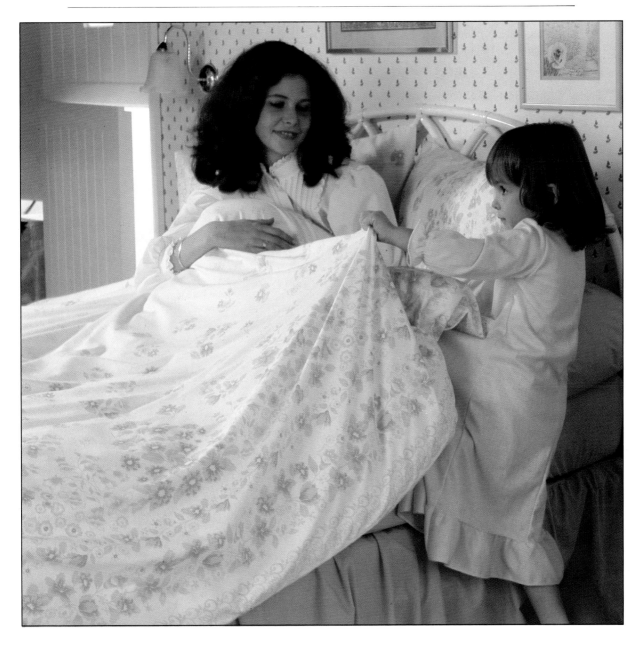

There is a lot to be said in favour of using a duvet. It is light and warm, and time spent on bed-making is minimal. Duvets are also the answer when you have awkwardly placed beds or when bedrooms are very small. In both cases the duvet is an excellent alternative to blankets but, more than that, with a smart cover it can transform the look of the room.

Duvet covers are very simple to make. They are just large fabric bags with a fastened opening set in the bottom or side edge. A side opening is useful in situations where the bed end is visible when you enter the bedroom and a fastened end would show.

How to make a simple duvet cover

WHAT YOU NEED
1 Sheeting fabric
2 Length of press fastening tape
Plus: Large cutting-out and small sewing scissors, matching and tacking thread, pins, needles.
NOTE Press fastener tape can be bought with metal or plastic fasteners; either type would be suitable for making duvet covers. When stitching in the press fastening tape, use a zipper foot, if you have one, on the sewing-machine as it can stitch close alongside the press fasteners.

HOW TO WORK OUT YOUR QUANTITIES
Duvet covers come in two main sizes: 140cm × 200cm for a single duvet and 200cm × 200cm for a double duvet—good sizes to follow. Make covers for cots to size 100cm × 120cm, with a 60cm opening; king-size duvets to 230cm × 220cm, with a 170cm opening.

When cutting out, allow 6.5cm for the base hem and 1.5cm for all seam allowances on both double and single covers. The opening size on a double duvet cover is 140cm; on a single it is 100cm.

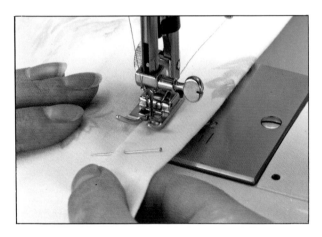

1 From fabric cut out two cover pieces to correct size. Fold a double 2.5cm wide hem along bottom edge of each piece for the opening edges. Pin, tack and stitch each hem

2 Place cover pieces with right sides together, matching base hem edges. Pin, tack and stitch together alongside the hem for 30cm in from each side, leaving a central opening

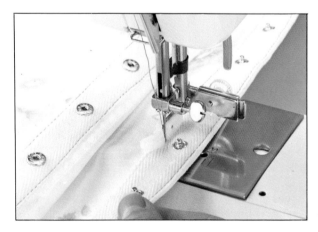

3 Tack one half of fastener tape centrally to hem, one side of opening. Tack second half of tape to opposite side of opening with fasteners matching. Stitch the long edges

4 With right sides together and hem edges matching, stitch across hems at each end of the opening, enclosing raw edges of fastener tape. Fasten off stitching securely

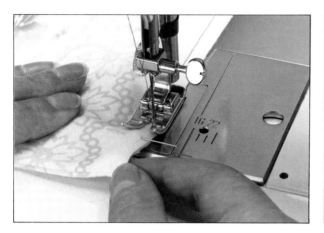

5 Stitch the two sides of cover with French seams. Make these by folding cover with wrong sides together, matching edges. Pin, tack and stitch sides, taking 5mm seam

6 To complete seam, turn cover, so right sides are together. Pin, tack and stitch sides again, taking 1cm seam allowance; and enclosing raw edges. Repeat, to stitch top edge. Turn

General hints

Duvet covers should be washed as frequently as sheets, so choose easy-care fabrics that need little or no ironing. Also, keep to colourfast fabrics and avoid home-dyed ones that cannot be washed with other items.

The most practical fabric to use for a duvet cover is sheeting, which comes in cotton or cotton and polyester mix and in very wide widths—178cm, 228cm and 275cm—so even double-size duvet covers can be made without seams across the width. Sheeting is available in a range of patterns as well as a good choice of plain colours.

Dress fabrics can be used for duvet covers, too. These are not so hardwearing or as wide as sheeting, but they provide a good alternative and add to the choice of patterns. Use the fabric so that the pattern helps to disguise the seams—for example, alternate broad bands of contrasting fabric—or even make the seams part of the overall design by trimming with contrasting braid.

However, avoid using fine cottons such as lawn as the duvet will show through the cover and the delicate fabric will not be able to support the weight of the fasteners.

Use French seams as they will enclose all raw edges making the seams strong and durable. Also, choose a strong fastener to keep the duvet neatly concealed inside the cover. Press fastener tape, which has press fasteners welded into the tape at 5cm intervals is a good type to use. Alternatives such as touch-and-close fastening, single press fasteners, zips, ribbon ties or buttons and buttonholes can also be used and the last two will add to the overall design of the cover.

Duvets for summer

If you are used to sleeping under a duvet but find it too warm in summer, why not change your duvet with the seasons and make a lightweight one with sheeting and terylene wadding?

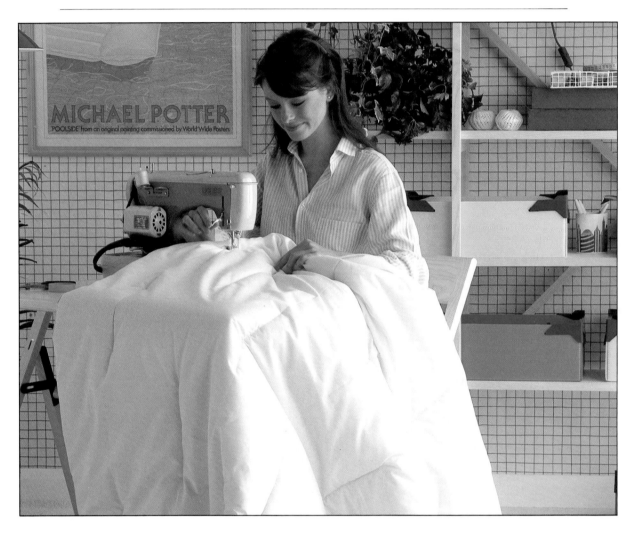

uvets which are so cozy in winter can often be too warm on summer nights. Having a lightweight summer duvet is the ideal alternative to going back to sheets and blankets. The single duvet shown here is simple to make and can be run up in an afternoon.

This duvet is made to standard measurements of 140cm×200cm. Known as 'step stitched', it is made by enclosing the wadding filling between two fabric layers and stitching all round the edge. The edges are then bound in strips of the same fabric and the duvet is quilted in stepped lines, 20cm in length.

Always use pale fabrics for a duvet so it will not show through the cover. This duvet is made in ordinary sheeting fabric—you can use either a cotton and polyester mixture or pure cotton—and is filled with a heavy-weight terylene wadding, materials which should all be available at any department store. It is best to use sheeting fabric because the wide width means there is no need for seams across the duvet. Finally, a sheeting duvet, filled with terylene wadding, is very easy to launder.

Once finished, slip your duvet into a bright new duvet cover. For instructions on making duvet covers and some ideas about fabrics to use see pages 39-41.

How to make a step-stitched duvet

WHAT YOU NEED

1 Plain wide-width cotton or cotton-polyester fabric

2 Heavyweight wadding

Plus: Cutting-out and small sewing scissors, matching and tacking thread, pins, needles, tape measure, metre stick, marking pencil or tailor's chalk

NOTE If you cannot buy wide-width fabric, join standard width fabric together with flat fell seams (see page 12) to gain the correct width. If you need to use two widths of fabric, double the fabric amount, see right.

HOW TO WORK OUT YOUR QUANTITIES

The standard size of a single duvet is 140cm × 200cm, so for this duvet you will need two pieces to this size. As the edges are bound, there is no need to add seam allowance to either the width or the length measurements.

For binding the edges, you will need sufficient 4cm-wide bias strips, so that when they are joined they will bind the entire outer edge. As the duvet is always covered with an attractive cover when on the bed, it will not matter if there are several joins in the binding round the outer edge.

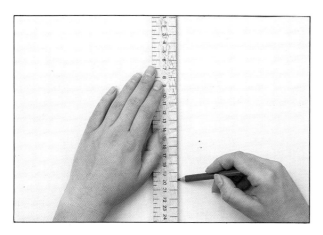

1 From fabric, cut out two pieces to the required size. Mark the quilting lines 20cm long with 36cm gaps in between. Begin and end 8cm from short edges. Graduate each row

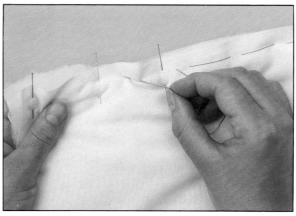

2 Take wadding the required size and place between the two pieces of fabric with wrong sides facing. Pin and tack together round the outer edge and across the duvet at intervals

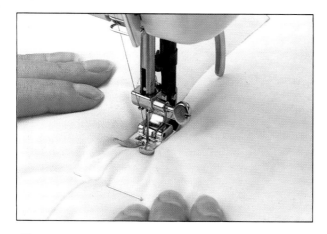

3 With a larger-than-average stitch, work quilting lines across the duvet, following marked lines and working from centre outwards. Work back stitches at each end of stitching

4 To give the duvet a firm edge, before binding round the outer edge, pin, tack and stitch through all three layers. Trim off excess wadding after stitching

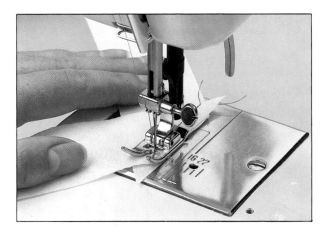

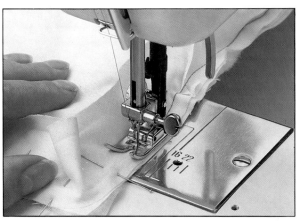

5 For binding, cut out 4cm-wide bias strips, which when stitched together will be long enough to go round the outer edge. Join strips together with plain flat seams

6 Fold in both raw edges on binding strip for 5mm and press. Open out one fold and place to one side of duvet, pin, tack and stitch to duvet through pressed crease

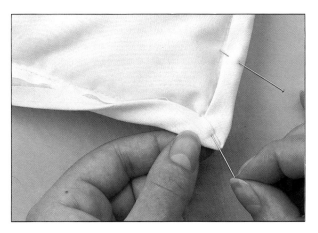

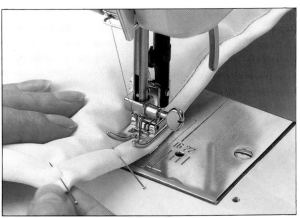

7 Join binding together to fit with a plain flat seam. Fold binding over the outer edge to the opposite side. On both sides of each corner fold the binding into a neat mitre

8 Pin, tack and stitch binding in place close to fold edge, round complete duvet, pivoting the needle at corners to make a neat right angle of stitching and to keep mitres in place

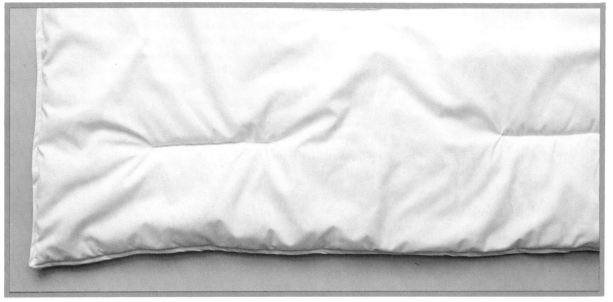

Gathered valances

Valances combine with duvets or bedspreads to give a neat and attractive finish to your bed

The finishing touch to a co-ordinating set of bed linen is made by the valance. It is essential on a divan, as it conceals the base and legs when it is used with fitted sheets and duvets.

The valance is made up from a main panel, cut to the size of the bed, and a flounced border which goes round the bottom and sides of the bed only, and is slipped between the mattress and the base of the bed so the flounce hangs just short of the floor. This type of valance needs less frequent laundering than the rest of the bed linen and so can be made to match other fabrics in the room, such as curtains, as well as—or instead of—matching the rest of the bedding. For economy, use patterned sheeting for a border and plain fabric for the centre panel under the mattress which won't show.

HOW TO MEASURE YOUR BED

When measuring a bed, remove all the bed clothes. Using a tape measure, measure the length of the mattress from the top edge to the bottom edge (C-D in the diagram on the right). Measure the width of the mattress from one side edge to the other (A-B in the diagram). Measure the distance from the top of the base to the floor (E-F in the diagram).

Calculate the cutting size for the main panel by adding 3.5cm to the length of the mattress and 3cm to the width. For the flounce, add 6.5cm to the height from the top of the base to the floor, to give the depth of flounce. Cut sufficient strips to this depth so that when joined they equal four times the length of the mattress plus twice the width, plus 4cm for top side hems.

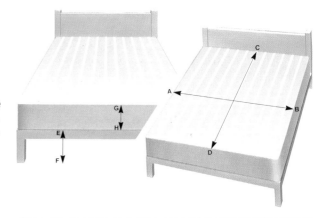

Above right: Measuring bed for main panel—A-B is the width, C-D the length
Measuring depth from top of base to floor (E-F) for flounce

BED SIZE (cm)	VALANCE in plain fabric (cm)	VALANCE in patterned fabric (cm)
Single		
75 × 190	280 × 228	360 × 228*
90 × 190	280 × 228	400 × 228*
Double		
135 × 190	320 × 228	400 × 228*
King-size		
150 × 200	370 × 228	410 × 228*

*On fabrics with a distinct pattern, allow five extra pattern repeats for matching the flounce pieces.

How to make a valance

WHAT YOU NEED
Sheeting fabric
Plus: Cutting-out and small sewing scissors, tape measure, metre rule, tacking and matching thread, pins, needles and tailor's chalk or a water-soluble marking pen.

HOW TO WORK OUT YOUR QUANTITIES
The chart (left) shows fabric quantities for valances for standard single, double and king size beds. Quantities for patterned fabric allow for cutting the main panel or sheet section on the lengthwise grain of the fabric, and all the flounce pieces in the same direction across the width of the fabric. If the fabric pattern is very distinctive, it will be necessary to match the flounce widths, so when you buy the fabric, allow an extra five pattern repeats for matching the pattern. Ladder stitch the fabric widths together (see page 12) to make sure that the pattern matches perfectly. However if the pattern is small, you will not need to match the widths, since gathers will hide the seams.

Measure your bed as shown in the diagram opposite to calculate the cutting sizes for the main panel of the valance and the flounce. If your bed is not a standard size, calculate the amount of fabric needed from the cutting sizes of the pieces.

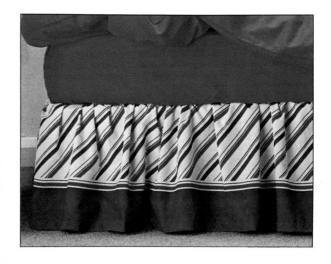

1 Mark out the main panel on the lengthways grain of the fabric. Curve the two corners at the base of the panel by drawing round the edge of a tea plate. Cut out main panel

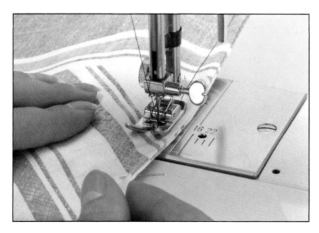

2 Measure and mark out the pieces for the flounce on the remaining fabric (see opposite). Cut out strips and join into one length with French seams (page 41), taking 1.5cm seam

3 Press 2.5cm to wrong side at lower hem edge of flounce. Turn a further 2.5cm to wrong side to make a double hem and pin, tack and stitch close to inner folded edge

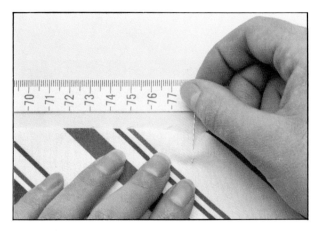

4 Divide by six the total length of the three edges of the main panel to which the flounce will be attached, and mark the six equal divisions with tailor's chalk or pins

5 In the same way, divide the length of the flounce into six and mark. Work two rows of gathering stitches, stopping and restarting the stitching at each mark

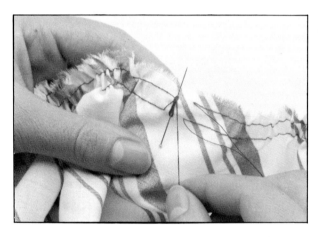

6 Evenly pull up the six lengths of gathering threads on the flounce to fit the sections round bottom and sides of the main panel. Secure thread ends by winding round a pin

7 With right sides together, raw edges level, and ends of flounce to top edges of main panel, pin flounce to panel, carefully matching up the six sections

8 Tack and stitch flounce to main panel. Trim seam allowance down to 1cm; stitch again and then zigzag stitch the raw edges together to neaten them

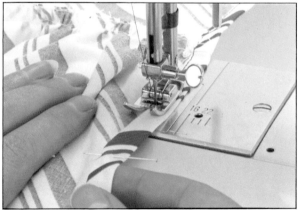

9 Press neatened seam on to main panel. Press a double 1cm hem to wrong side along side edges of flounce and top raw edge of main panel; pin, tack and stitch

Pleated valances

Even-sized box-pleats along a valance will give a crisp, tailored finish to a bed. Or, if you want to economize on fabric, you can create a similar effect by using simple, inverted corner pleats

A smart alternative to the more commonly used gathered valance is a pleated design. Box–pleated valances always look crisp and hang well, yet they are no more expensive and just as easy to make as the gathered type. Because they hang flush to the sides of the bed they look particularly good in twin-bedded rooms.

For a box-pleated valance, it is best to choose a fabric with a pattern that does not get 'lost' in the pleating. Fabrics with stripes or small, all-over patterns, are most suitable. If you want to achieve the same effect as a box-pleated valance but use less fabric, you can make a straight-sided valance with inverted pleats at the two bottom corners only. Two fabrics are used for this valance, the main fabric and a secondary one which forms the inverted pleat. The second fabric could be left over from making curtains, cushions or other bedding.

How to make a box-pleated valance

WHAT YOU NEED
Sheeting fabric
Plus: Cutting-out and small sewing scissors, tape measure, metre rule, tacking and matching thread, pins, needles, tailor's chalk or a water-soluble marking pen.

Try to pick a wide-width sheeting fabric: 228cm – 274cm wide to avoid joins in the valance. An ideal choice is a fabric that does not have a one-way design and has a small pattern repeat to match. Remember that the valance will be on show with the rest of your bed-linen, so choose harmonizing fabric.

HOW TO WORK OUT YOUR QUANTITIES
Refer to page 46 and 47 for how to measure your bed and for a guide to fabric quantities. For the pleated valance work out the number and size of pleats that can be fitted into the bed length, and, if it amounts to an odd figure, make the two pleats on either side at the top of the bed slightly larger or smaller, as in this position, they'll be less obvious. Also, arrange for pleats to meet at bottom corners. On a standard double bed— 135cm × 190cm—a good size for the pleats is 13.5cm, with the last pleats at the top 14.5cm.

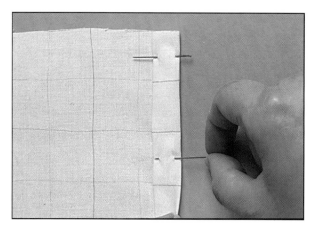

1 Mark and cut out the main panel piece to the required size as Step 1, page 47. Turn under a double 1.5cm hem along the top edge. Pin, tack and stitch the top hem in place

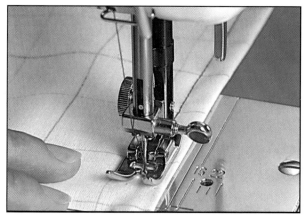

2 Cut out the required number of fabric widths for the flounce and join strips together with narrow French seams to gain the correct length for the entire bed, Step 2, page 47

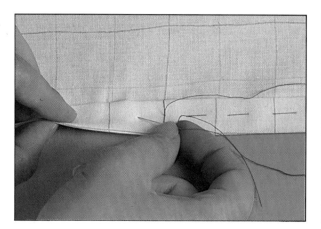

3 Turn under a 1.5cm hem on short ends of flounce. Turn under hem again for 1.5cm, to form a double hem. Pin, tack and stitch hem in place

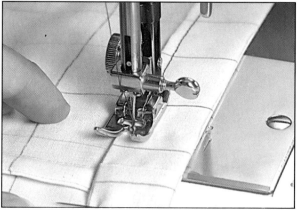

4 Turn under 2.5cm and then a further 2.5cm to form a double hem along one long edge of the flounce strip. Pin, tack and stitch hem in place, step 3, page 47

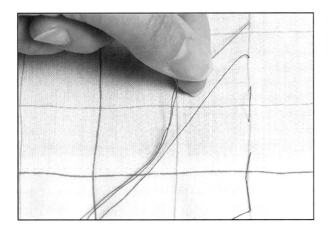

5 Fold the flounce strip in half widthways, matching short edges together. Mark position of the centre fold of flounce strip with a row of tacking stitches in a contrasting thread

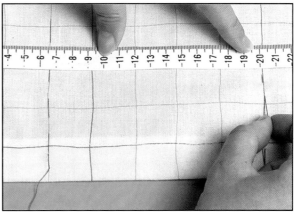

6 For the first pleat, working from tacked centre line to one side, mark a fold line 6.75cm away and again 6.75cm away. Mark a 13.5cm wide box pleat, then two more fold lines

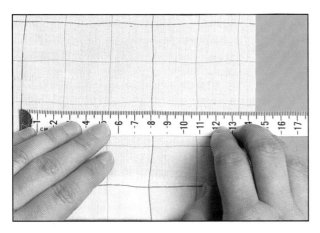

7 Continue making pleat lines and fold lines along flounce. Repeat to end along opposite side of tacked centre line. At each end mark the last pleat 14.5cm wide

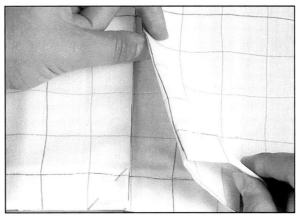

8 To make pleats, fold the pleat inwards along first fold line to meet the tacked central line. Pin at top and bottom of pleat to hold firmly in place

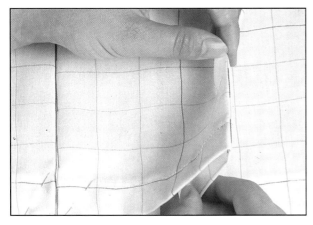

9 Fold the pleat in reverse direction on the opposite side of the central point. Pin firmly to hold. Repeat Steps 8 and 9 in turn to pleat up the complete flounce

10 Right sides together, pin pleated flounce to base, positioning a pleat at each corner point. Tack and stitch together, taking 1.5cm seams. Zigzag raw edges together

51

CUSHIONS & SEATING

Cushion pads and covers

A scattering of colourful cushions can transform the look of a room at little cost. And once you've decided the size, filling and fabric cover you want, you can make them up in a single evening!

Cushions not only make a sofa or chair look more inviting, they add a general feeling of comfort to a room. And, they can be decorative as well as practical, especially when fabrics are chosen carefully to introduce new colours into a room, or to blend with the existing colour scheme.

Cushion pads are available in a range of sizes—or make your own, following the instructions here.

Plain covers for square or rectangular cushions are easy to make. Many types of fabric can be used, although the choice will depend on where the cushions are to be used and how much wear they will have. Cushions for a bedroom, for instance, can be made in lacy fabrics, voile or satins, while those for a living room need a more hard-wearing fabric such as furnishing cotton. Always choose washable fabric.

The step-by-step instructions also show ways of fastening a cover, and how to apply piping and decorative edges.

Choosing fillings

Down, feathers, feathers-and-down
These make beautifully soft cushions, but must be enclosed in special down-proof cambric or feather-proof ticking to prevent the feathers escaping from the cushion. (Two rows of stitching along the seam also help prevent this.)

Foam
Foam chips, shredded foam and crumbled foam are all names for the same type of inexpensive synthetic filling. Foam is not absorbent, so it is not suitable for children's cushions, or for garden use. Always fill the cushion pad so that the foam is tightly packed to avoid lumpiness.

Polyester wadding
This matted fibre is slightly more expensive than foam, but less lumpy, and is also washable, so it is suitable for use outdoors or in children's rooms.

Kapok
Kapok is a vegetable fibre, and slightly more expensive than its polyester equivalent. Although soft, it is non-absorbent and tends to go lumpy after a few years use.

How to work out your quantities
The amount of filling needed will depend on the type used and the size of the cushion. An average-size cushion (45-50cm square) will take approximately 350g down, 900g feathers, or 700-800g of one of the synthetic or vegetable fillings.

Cover fabrics
For fillings like foam chips, kapok and polyester wadding, you can use calico, curtain lining fabric or even good areas of old, worn-out cotton sheets for the pad cover.

How to make a simple cushion pad

WHAT YOU NEED

1 Fabric suitable for pad cover
2 Filling
Plus: Cutting-out and small sewing scissors, tape measure, tacking and matching thread, dressmaker's pins, needles
NOTE Before you buy, check that fabric and filling are compatible—a down- or feather-proof fabric is essential for a feather-and-down filling. And, when using a coloured foam filling make sure that the cushion-pad fabric will mask the colour so the filling will not show through to the right side of the pad.

HOW TO WORK OUT YOUR QUANTITIES

Decide on the size of the cushion and add 3cm seam allowance to both the width and the length. You will need two pieces of fabric this size for each cushion pad. The quantity of fabric required will depend on the size of the cushion and the width of the fabric you are using. The most economical way of cutting out the pieces is side by side across the width of the fabric, where this is possible. Alternatively, if this is not possible, cut out cushion pads of different sizes, side by side across the fabric width.

1 Cut out two pieces of fabric to the size required. Turn 1.5cm to the wrong side along one side of each piece and press in the fold. Pin to hold in place

2 Place the two pieces of fabric wrong sides together and sew French seams (page 41) along the two edges adjoining the folded edge, taking a 1.5cm seam allowance

3 With wrong sides together, sew a French seam on the remaining edge, turning the already completed seams in towards the centre when stitching, for a neat corner

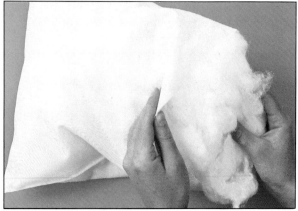

4 Turn right side out and press. Insert filling until pad is sufficiently plump. Pin and tack the edges of the opening together and machine stitch close to the edge

How to make a simple cushion cover

WHAT YOU NEED
Furnishing fabric
Plus: Cutting-out and small sewing scissors, tape measure, tacking and matching thread, dressmaker's pins, needles

HOW TO WORK OUT YOUR QUANTITIES
For a really good fit a cushion cover should be slightly smaller than the cushion pad it is covering. Measure the pad from one side seam to the other in both directions, deduct 1.5cm from each measurement; then add 3cm seam allowance to both measurements.

The amount of fabric you will require depends on the size of the cushion and the width of the fabric being used. It will also vary if the fabric has a bold design which you wish to feature in the centre of the cover. On plain fabrics or those with an indistinct design or small pattern repeat, two pieces can usually be cut side by side across the width. With distinct designs or large patterns you may need extra fabric to obtain a whole repeat.
NOTE See page 57 for estimating quantities for decorative trimmings such as piping, frills and zigzag or scalloped edges.

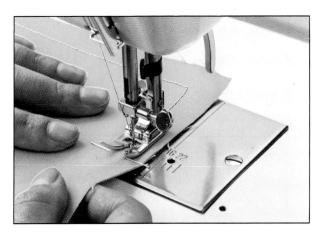

1 Cut two pieces of fabric to the required size. Place right sides together and pin, tack and stitch all round, taking a 1.5cm seam allowance; leave central opening in one side

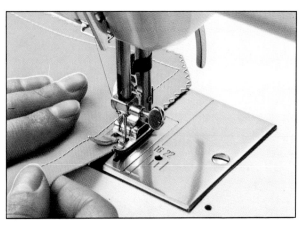

2 Trim the seam allowance to 1cm and clip across the corners to reduce bulk. Neaten the raw edges together with a medium-width zigzag stitch and turn to the right side

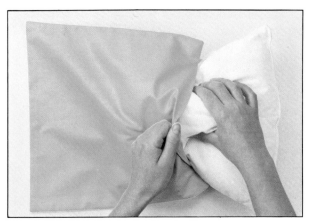

3 Zigzag raw edges of opening. Turn 1.5cm to the wrong side along both edges of opening. Insert cushion pad, pushing the corners right into the corners of cover

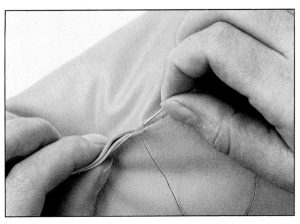

4 Pin the folded edges together along the remaining side and slipstitch together using a matching sewing thread. Fasten off the stitching and plump up the cushion

TG127·33

Choosing and applying fastenings

To achieve an evenly-shaped cushion cover, slipstitch the opening closed, as shown on **page 55**. However, the opening will have to be undone and restitched every time the cover is removed for laundering. To make the cushion cover easy to remove for laundering, fasten with a zip, touch-and-close fastenings, or press fasteners.

Choose a light- to medium-weight metal zip which is 10cm shorter than the shortest side of the cushion. Touch-and-close fastening is available by the metre or as small spots. If buying by the metre, choose a light-weight variety to tone with the colour of the cushion cover. Spots also come in different colours, and these can be trimmed down to a smaller size. Metal or nylon press fasteners can be used. When using these three alternative fastenings, add an extra 3cm seam allowance to the fastening side of the cover.

1 Fold 1.5cm to wrong side, stitch. Fold over again. Stitch alongside hem leaving central opening

2a **To apply touch-and-close spots,** stitch pairs of spots along folded hem at opening at regular intervals

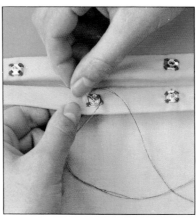

2b **To apply press fasteners**, blanket stitch the two halves to corresponding points along the opening

3 Unfasten. Pin, tack and stitch remaining sides, taking 1.5cm seam. Catch in folded hem. Neaten with zigzag as **page 55**.

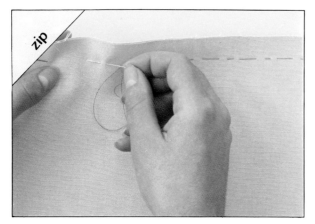

1 To prepare for a zip fastener, place pieces right sides together; pin, and tack along one side. Stitch in from each end, leaving a central opening. Tack opening edges together

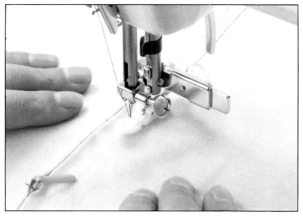

2 To insert a zip fastener, place the zip face down on the seam allowances over the tacked part of the seam. Pin, tack and stitch zip in place from the right side

Decorative trimmings

Cushion covers can be trimmed in a number of ways. **Piping** is a popular way of trimming a cushion and gives extra strength to the edges. It is made by covering the cotton piping cord in fabric to match or contrast with the cushion cover. **Frills** are made from double thickness so that they look good from both sides. Fabric is folded in half lengthways, wrong sides together, and raw edges gathered together, to give a double thickness frill. **Scalloped or zigzag edgings** can be made by stitching two lengths of fabric right sides together around the shape and turning right side out. All of these trimmings are inserted between the two cushion pieces and stitched in place with the main cushion seams.

HOW TO WORK OUT YOUR QUANTITIES
Measure round all four sides of cover.
For piping, add 5cm for length of piping cord required. Cut strips of fabric for piping on the bias grain, wide enough to enclose the cord, plus 3cm seams.
For double frills, join lengths of bias fabric, twice the frill depth plus 3cm for seam allowances, and join to make double the total cushion measurement.
For zigzag and scalloped edgings cut eight lengths of fabric the length of the cushion sides. Allow 6.5cm for mitred corners to the desired depth of the edging, plus 3cm for the seam allowances (see page 58).

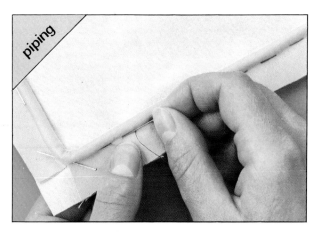

1 For piped cushions, prepare piping (see pages 64-5). Pin and tack to right side of one cushion piece, joining at the centre of one edge and clipping seam allowance at corners

2 Stitch in place using a zipper foot or piping attachment to enable you to stitch really close to the cord. Complete the cushion cover Steps 1-4, page 55

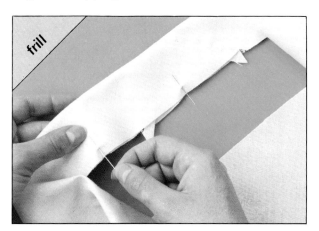

1 For a 3cm-wide double frill, cut fabric strips 9cm wide and join to make double the length of outer edge. Join short edges to make a ring. Fold in half lengthways, wrong sides together

2 Work two rows of gathering stitches through both fabric layers. Pull up gathers. Pin, tack and stitch to right side of one cushion piece. Complete Steps 1-4, page 55

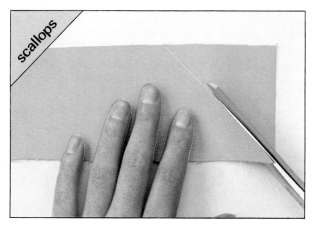

1 For a 4cm-wide scalloped border, cut eight 7cm-wide lengths of fabric 6.5cm longer than finished sides. Graduate sides: mark 8cm along base. Cut from top corners to this mark

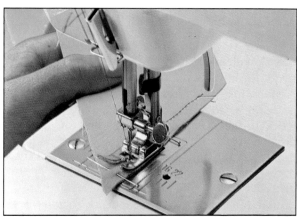

2 Place two border pieces, right sides together; pin, tack and stitch to within 1.5cm of bottom edge, taking 1.5cm seam allowance. Press open. Repeat to complete border

3 Make pattern of one finished side. Divide equally into scallops, with half a scallop at each end. Mark scallop pattern carefully on wrong side of each fabric piece in turn

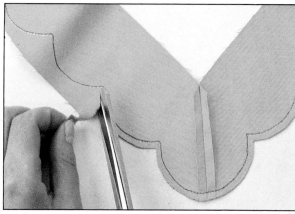

4 Make up second border piece in the same way, Steps 2 and 3. Place with right side to first set. Stitch round scallops. Trim and clip between scallops. Turn to right side

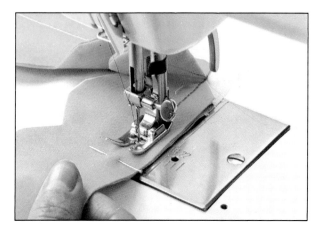

5 Pin base edges of border together, 1.5cm from edge. Position border to right side of one piece, matching seams to corners. Pin, tack and stitch. Complete Steps 1-4, page 55

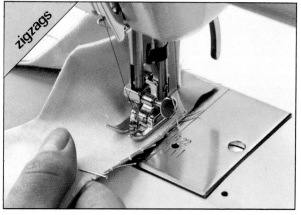

1 For a 4cm-wide zigzag border, cut out fabric and join together as for scalloped border, Steps 1 and 2. Make a pattern and stitch border to cushion, as scalloped border Steps 3–5

How to make patchwork cushions

Cushions are perfect for showing off patchwork skills, and their small size and simple shape make them a good way to learn the craft. Once you've acquired the basic skills, you can apply the same techniques to larger items.

The cushions shown below are made using hand-sewn patchwork. Also known as English patchwork, this makes use of paper templates, around which the pieces of fabric are tacked. After the edges of the pieces have been sewn together by hand, the templates are removed.

English patchwork traditionally uses four shapes—squares, triangles, diamonds and hexagons. Each of these is featured in one of the cushions shown here, and the patterns for the templates are given on this page. Most patchwork designs are made up of just one of the four shapes, but you can also combine shapes, such as squares with triangles. Designs which use more than one shape are called pieced blocks.

The step-by-step instructions show you how to make up English patchwork. Select the pattern that most appeals to you, or create your own, then follow the steps to make up your patchwork fabric. The edges on some designs will be uneven, but so long as you leave a minimum 5mm seam allowance, you can treat the patchwork fabric the same as any other fabric with a large design. If you want to pipe the cushions, follow the instructions on page 57.

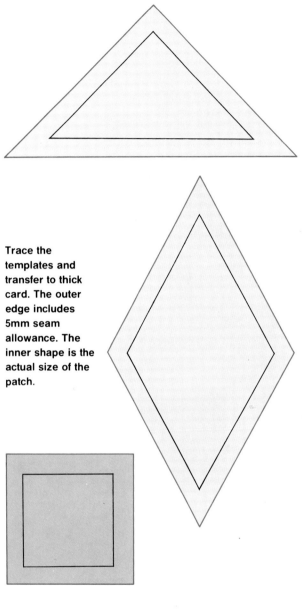

Trace the templates and transfer to thick card. The outer edge includes 5mm seam allowance. The inner shape is the actual size of the patch.

WHAT YOU NEED

To make one cushion about 30cm square:
1 Cutting board
2 Thick paper or thin card
3 Thick card
4 Graph paper
5 Felt-tipped pens
6 Craft knife
7 Pencil
8 Straight edge or steel ruler
9 Fabrics in different colourways
10 Fabric for back of cushion
11 Cushion pad 30cm×30cm
12 Set square (or use a square object)
Plus: Tacking thread, toning threads, needle, pins, scissors, tape measure, masking tape

HOW TO WORK OUT YOUR QUANTITIES

Here are the number of patches you will need for each fabric; the letters are to show you which fabrics are used in more than one cushion. Square sampler cushion: 20 patches from fabric A, 16 from B, 16 from H and 57 from I. Diamond sampler cushion: 25 patches from fabric A, and 27 each from B and C. Hexagon sampler cushion: 10 patches from fabric E, 17 from H, and 19 from I. Triangle sampler cushion: 18 patches from fabric D, and 12 each from F and J, plus four 2.75cm-wide strips each of fabrics D, F and G (two of each 23.5cm long and two 20cm long).

Using the templates on page 59, draw a plan of the patches for each fabric, then measure the overall dimensions.

1 Using graph paper, draw out all of the designs and try out possible colour combinations with coloured felt-tipped pens or fabric scraps (see page 102, Steps 1a and 1b)

2 Make templates for each shape, to include a 5mm seam allowance all round (see page 59 for patterns). make a second set, actual size of the finished patch, in a different colour

3 Add up the number of patches you will need for each shape to be used. Carefully trace round the smaller templates on to thin card or thick paper and cut out the numbers you need

4 Lay the larger, thick template on wrong side of fabric and trace round with lead pencil. Butt templates up to lines to avoid waste. Cut out all the fabric patches

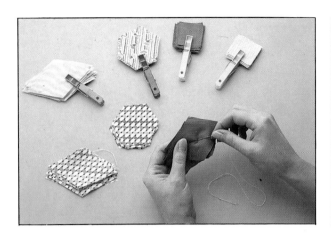

5 To store the patchwork pieces, knot one end of a length of tacking thread for each shape and colour and string them together. Alternatively, peg them together

6 Place paper template on wrong side of fabric. Pin template to patch. Use two or three pins to hold if necessary. You should have an even seam allowance all round

7a **On smaller patches,** fold edges over and tack through paper, folding neat corners as you go. Use small tacking stitches and make sure that you sew through the corners

7b **On larger patches,** tape down edges before tacking. Cut out several strips of tape in readiness. Remove pins and press edges on wrong side to give a sharp sewing line

8 Right sides together, and using small oversewing stitches join the patches checking pattern as you go. Catch the stitches on fabric only, not on the template

9 Join triangles in strips. Work hexagons and squares in strips or clusters. Join diamonds in clusters. Remove all tacking and tape. Proceed as Steps 1-4, page 55

61

Simple gusseted cushions

Large square cushions with gussets make a comfortable seat for a wooden or cane chair. Alternatively use the gusset strip to enhance smaller round or square cushions with soft gathers

imple square or round cushions can be given a box shape by inserting a gusset strip between the two main sections of the cushion. Large square gusseted cushions make ideal seat cushions, especially for non-upholstered seats, as the added cushion depth that the gusset allows gives the extra comfort needed.

Adding gussets to the basic cushion shape opens up possibilities of combining different fabrics for a decorative effect. Contrasting fabrics can be used for gusset and main cover for instance, or you could use the same fabric design for both but in different colourways.

Cushion gussets can be gathered for a softer look. They may also be edged with a piping.

As with other kinds of cushion covers, it is best to make gusseted covers slightly smaller than the cushion pad to give the cushion a firm, plump appearance. You can make your own cushion pad to size by following the instructions for covers below and omitting the zips, but if you choose to buy one ready-made, it is worth remembering that you do not have to follow the exact dimensions of the pad itself. To increase the gusset width of the cover, simply reduce the size of the top and base cover pieces and the pad will fill out to fit the cover.

How to make a piped gusseted cushion

WHAT YOU NEED

1 Fabric
2 Zip, 16cm longer than one cushion side
3 Piping cord
4 Square cushion pad with gusset
Plus: Cutting-out and small sewing scissors, tacking and matching threads, pins, needles, tape measure

HOW TO WORK OUT YOUR QUANTITIES

To calculate the amount of fabric needed for the cushion measure the cushion pad. The fabric amount will also depend on the fabric width and whether the fabric design needs to be centred on the cushion top. Measure the cushion pad top both ways and add 3cm to both measurements for seam allowance. The gusset is divided up into four pieces: the front, two sides and one back piece, which encloses the zip that extends round the two back corners to give a wider opening. For the front gusset measure the length and width of one cushion side and add 3cm to both measurements for seam allowance. For back gusset measure one side of cushion pad. Add 19cm to the length and 6cm to the width to allow for zip opening. For side gussets measure the length and width of one cushion side. Deduct 8cm from the length and add 3cm to the width for seam allowance. For piping, measure round cushion top, double the measurement and add 10cm.

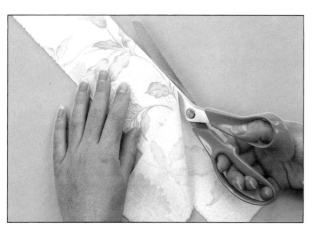

1 Cut out cushion top and base. Cut out one front, one back and two side gussets to the required size. Cut back gusset in half lengthways: fold gusset in half; cut along fold

2 For piping cut 5cm-wide bias strips which, when joined together, will fit twice round gusset. Pin, tack and stitch strips together taking 1.5cm seam allowance

3 Place cord to wrong side along centre of bias strip. Fold strip in half, enclosing cord. Pin, tack and stitch close to cord down complete length of strip, using a zipper foot

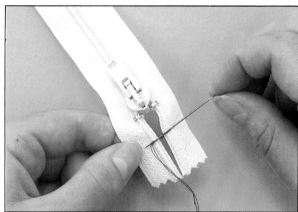

4 Hand stitch the tape ends at top and bottom of zip together so they lie flat and will not part. Turn 1.5cm to the wrong side on centre edges of back gusset and press

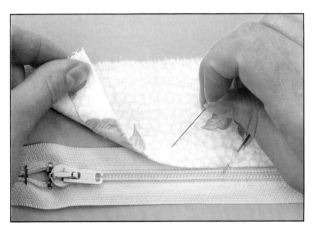

5 To insert an exposed zip, place the folded edges of back gusset close to the zip teeth. Pin, tack and stitch the gusset to the zip, finishing at the end of each side of the zip

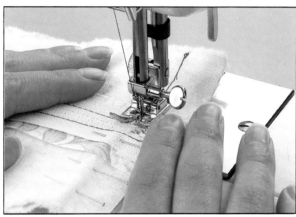

6 With right sides facing, pin the gussets together with side gussets in between front and back gussets. Tack and stitch, leaving 1.5cm open at each end of front/side seam

7 Beginning at the centre of the back edges, place covered piping on the right side of cushion top and base, 1.5cm from outer edge. Pin and tack, clipping into fabric at corners

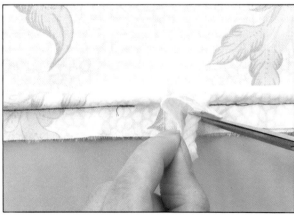

8 Beginning 1cm from end of piping, stitch covered piping in place all round to within 2cm of opposite end. Trim cord to meet first end and trim fabric to 1cm beyond cord end

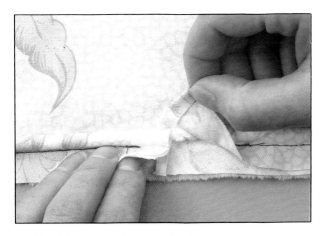

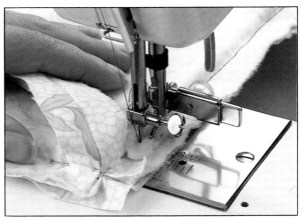

9 Fold fabric end under for 6mm then wrap round beginning of piping with cord ends meeting. Stitch across the join, overlapping previous stitching by 1cm on either side

10 Pin, tack and stitch the gusset to the top of the cushion cover, matching front seams with corners. Open zip. Repeat, to stitch other edge of gusset to base. Turn to right side

How to make a round gusseted cushion

WHAT YOU NEED
1 Fabric in two harmonizing designs
2 Zip, one-third of the circumference
3 Round cushion pad with gusset
Plus: Cutting-out and small sewing scissors, matching and tacking thread, pins, needles, tape measure, brown paper, string, drawing pin, pencil, pinboard or large cork tile, household or craft paper scissors
NOTE Make up a paper pattern for the cushion pieces following Steps 1–4, pages 79-80. The pattern size can be altered to suit your requirements.

HOW TO WORK OUT YOUR QUANTITIES
Measure the diameter of the cushion pad and add 3cm seam allowance to give the cutting size. You will need two circles to this size. Remember to allow for a fabric with a distinctive design which will need to be centred on the cushion front and back. Measure the width of the gusset. Measure the circumference of the gusset and divide into three equal lengths. Add 3cm seam allowance to both width and length. You will need two gussets to this size and one gusset 3cm wider to allow for the zip opening.

1 Cut out two circles and three gusset pieces to the required size. Cut the zip gusset in half lengthways. Turn under 1.5cm allowance along cut edges of zip gusset and press

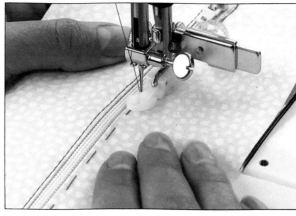

2 Stitch the top and bottom zip tape ends together as Step 4, page 64. Pin and tack zip gusset to zip with fold edge of fabric against zip teeth. Stitch close to fold

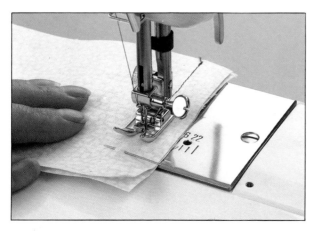

3 Place gussets with right sides together; pin, tack and stitch into a ring with plain flat seams. Clip into the seam allowance on both sides of the gusset ring, at 2.5cm intervals

4 Pin, tack and stitch gusset to front cover piece. Open zip. Repeat, to stitch back cover piece to opposite edge of gusset. Turn cover to right side through zip

How to make a gathered gusseted cushion

WHAT YOU NEED
1 Fabric in two harmonizing designs
2 Round cushion pad with gusset
Plus: Cutting-out and small sewing scissors, matching and tacking thread, pins, needles, tape measure

HOW TO WORK OUT YOUR QUANTITIES
Measure circumference of pad and width of gusset. Add 3cm seam allowance to top and base pieces. Add 3cm allowance to gusset width and allow two and a half times the circumference for gathering the gusset.

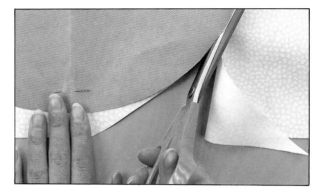

1 Make pattern to the required size (Steps 1-4, pages 79-80). Using pattern cut out cushion front and back. Cut gusset strips

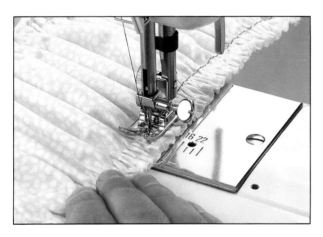

2 Pin, tack and stitch gusset into a ring. Work two rows of gathering stitches, 5mm and 7mm from each long edge of gusset. Pull up gathers to fit. Stitch over gathers

3 With right sides together, pin the gusset to cushion front; tack and stitch. Pin, tack and stitch opposite edge of gusset to cushion back, leaving an opening, one-third of circumference

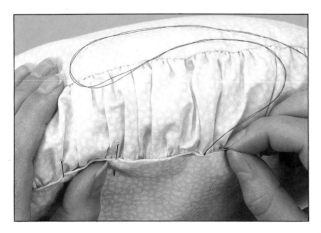

4 Trim and turn cushion cover to the right side. Insert cushion pad, turn in opening edges and pin to hold. Slipstitch opening edges together to close

How to make a square gusseted cushion

WHAT YOU NEED
1 Fabric
2 Square cushion pad with gusset
Plus: Cutting-out and small sewing
scissors, matching and tacking thread,
pins, needles, tape measure

HOW TO WORK OUT YOUR QUANTITIES
Measure the cushion pad both ways and
add 3cm to both measurements for seam
allowance. Measure the width and
circumference of gusset and add 3cm to
both measurements for seam allowance.

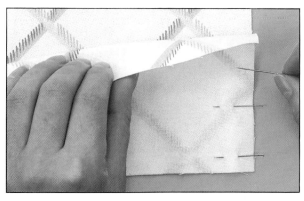

1 Cut out cushion pieces to required size. Pin,
and stitch gusset edges together with plain
flat seam, leaving 1.5cm open at each end

2 Place one long edge of gusset to cushion front with right sides together, matching gusset seam to one corner of the cushion front and clipping corner. Pin gusset in place to hold

3 Tack and stitch gusset to cushion front. Pin, tack and stitch opposite edge of gusset to cushion back in the same way, leaving an opening centrally in one side

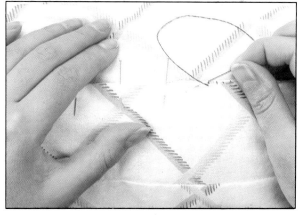

4 Trim and turn cushion cover to the right side. Insert the cushion pad into the cover. Turn in opening edges and slipstitch together with small invisible stitches to close

Covering a boxy shape

Easier to make than they look, loose covers can save you expense
when you wish to change your colour scheme but keep the same
furniture or give a new lease of life to a jaded or worn suite

Loose covers can be made to fit over most sofa and armchair shapes. They are an ideal way of adapting the furniture you already have to a new colour scheme with the additional advantage of being easily removable for cleaning. The simplest shape to cover is a square shape where you are working only with rectangles of fabric.

Although it is possible to buy paper patterns which give general cutting guides, you will get a far better fit by pinning the fabric to the sofa or chair itself, marking your stitching lines as you go and trimming the rectangles to fit the panels. You can add piping in the same or contrast fabric both to strengthen the cover and give it a neat finish. The lower skirt edge can be gathered, given a tailored look with box-pleats or pleated corners or made simply straight.

Left and above: Finish a plain, loose-covered sofa with a smart box-pleat skirt. Emphasize the clean-cut lines with self-covered piping cord, inserted into the seams when the cover pieces are stitched together

Choosing fabric

Choose a strong upholstery fabric—tough and firmly woven to give maximum wear. If the covers are to be washed, the fabric must also be colour-fast and non-shrink. Many fabrics are made especially for upholstery purposes— cotton, linen union and man-made fibres—but do not choose anything too thick as it will be bulky and difficult to sew.

If choosing a patterned fabric, try to pick an all-over or random design as these are more economical than a large pattern with a large motif, which must be centred. Be generous when estimating for your fabric; any spare fabric can be used to make matching scatter cushions or arm covers. If you are piping the cover, either use the same fabric or choose a contrast-colour of a similar weight.

For sofas you will need to join widths of fabric to make up the large pieces of the outside and inside back, the seat and the front border. When using large patterns, the best positions for the seams are on either side of the centre—use a whole width of fabric as a centre panel with equal-sized pieces joined to either side. (Remember to ladder stitch the fabrics together, as described on page 12, to get a perfect match at the seam lines.) Alternatively, you can line the seams up with the edges of the cushions.

Fitting the cover

To get a really good, close fit, you must pin-fit all the pieces together on the sofa before sewing them together. Add the skirt when the main cover has been completed.

A very important part of the cover is the tuck-in section which is allowed for at the back and sides of the seat. This excess fabric is tucked around the seat and anchors the cover in place.

How to measure

Measure each section and write down the dimensions in the spaces provided in the Key (below right). Also make a note of the direction of the warp (crossways) threads. Add 3cm (for seam allowances) or 18cm (for tuck-in and seams) to each measurement.

Decide on the style of skirt you want. For the pleated skirt on page 70, subtract 15cm from the height of the outside back (AB) and arms (EF), arm box strip (Z6Z7) and fron panel (WX). Measure all round the base of the sofa and double the measurement for the box pleats, allowing 3cm for seam allowances. Cut in 18cm-wide strips that, when joined together, will make up to the required measurement. See page 77 for other skirts.

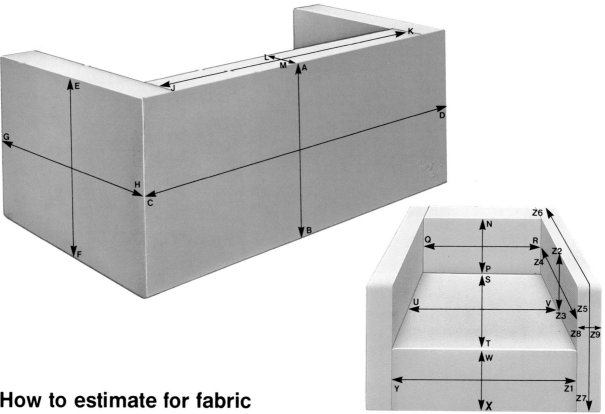

How to estimate for fabric

Use graph paper on which the large squares are subdivided into ten smaller squares. With each small square representing 1cm, draw the pattern pieces on to the graph paper following your measurements in the Key. Label each piece, mark the directions of the warp and cut out the pieces. On the same graph paper and using the same scale, draw a long rectangle to the width of your chosen fabric.

For plain fabrics, arrange the pattern pieces as close together as possible, keeping the warp square.

For patterned fabrics, mark in the length of the pattern repeat or where the main motifs fall, so that you can centre the pattern on each piece.

To find the total length of fabric needed, measure length of the plan and convert it back from the scale. If you are piping the cover, use the areas of fabric between pattern pieces or add extra fabric.

AB	Outside back height =	+3cm =	
CD	Outside back length =	+3cm =	
EF	Outside arm height =	+3cm =	
GH	Outside arm length =	+3cm =	
JK	Back box strip length =	+3cm =	
LM	Back box strip width =	+3cm =	
NP	Inside back height =	+18cm =	
QR	Inside back width =	+3cm =	
ST	Seat length =	+18cm =	
UV	Seat width =	+18cm =	
WX	Front panel height =	+3cm =	
YZ1	Front panel length =	+3cm =	
Z2Z3	Inside arm height =	+18cm =	
Z4Z5	Inside arm length =	+3cm =	
Z6Z7	Arm box strip length =	+3cm =	
Z8Z9	Arm box strip width =	+3cm =	
	Cushion top/base length =	+3cm =	
	Cushion top/base width =	+3cm =	
	Gusset depth =	+3cm =	

How to fit and make the covers

WHAT YOU NEED

1 Fabric, suitable for loose covers
2 Hooks and eyes
3 Piping cord if desired
4 Cushion zips, see page 64
Plus: Cutting-out and small sewing scissors, tacking and matching threads, pins, needles, tape measure, metre ruler, tailor's chalk or marking pencil, graph paper.
NOTE If you are piping the cover, see page 77 before buying any piping cord. Piping is shown in detail on pages 64-5. You will need matching thread to join the bias strips.

HOW TO WORK OUT YOUR QUANTITIES

Measure your sofa or chair and draw up a cutting plan as instructed opposite. For the skirt fabric, first decide on the style of skirt (see page 77) and then follow the instructions opposite. If using piping cord, measure round each piece that needs to be piped and add the amounts together. Bias strips for covering the piping can be cut from the spare fabric.
NOTE A quick, but far less accurate, method of working out amount of 122cm-wide fabric is to multiply the outside back height by 5.

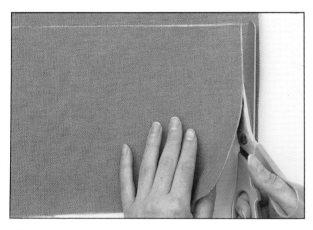

1 Lay the upholstery fabric on the floor, right side up. Mark out the pieces following the cutting chart as a guide (see opposite). Cut out each piece and label it

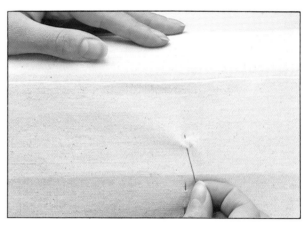

2 Using tailor's chalk or pins, mark centre of outside and inside back, seat and front border on the sofa. Repeat to mark the centre of the corresponding fabric pieces

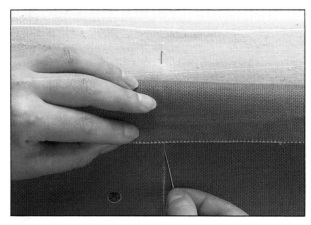

3 Fit outside back first: with wrong side out, pin fabric to sofa, matching centre lines with seam lines extending at top and base. Pin fabric to side edges

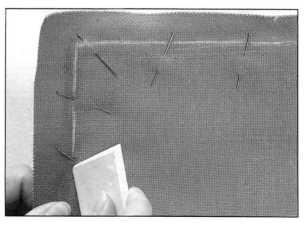

4 On the wrong side of the fabric, using tailor's chalk, mark in stitching lines along top edge and down sides of outside back. Use original upholstery as a guide

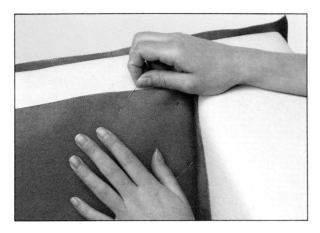

5 Position and pin the inside back in place with seam allowance extending at top. Leave 15cm tuck-in allowance free at base edge. Mark the stitching line as before

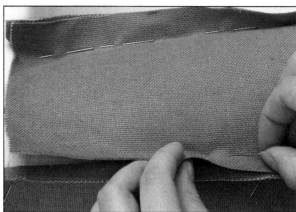

6 Place the back box strip to top of sofa and pin the inside and then outside back pieces to the box strip. Mark in stitching lines as before, trimming down seam if necessary

7 Pin the inside and outside arms in place with seam allowances extending. Pin outside back to one outside arm. Leave tuck-in allowance free on inside. Mark stitching lines

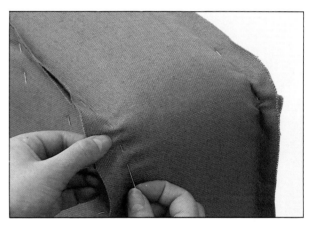

8 Pin the outside and inside arms to the arm box strip. Pin arm box strip to ends of back box strip. Trim seam allowances if necessary and mark in stitching lines

9 Position and pin the seat in place, matching centre to centre of sofa and round the edges along the tuck-in allowance. Mark along the front stitching line, trimming if necessary

10 To fit the tuck-in sections, first match the tuck-ins between the inside back and the arms. Then pin the tuck-ins together round the seat to inside arms and back

11 Unpin cover and stitch together with right sides together following marked seamlines. First stitch back and arm box strips together. Zigzag seam allowances to neaten

12 Continue to sew cover. Leave one edge of outside back open for about three-quarters of its length for fastenings. Snip into allowance where stitching ends at top of opening

13 Refit cover on sofa wrong side out and fit around the seat. Pin front panel to seat and arm pieces; mark stitching lines and trim seam allowance if necessary

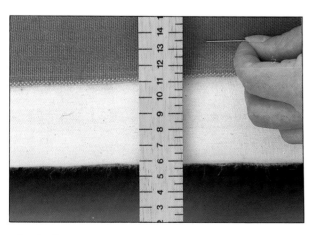

14 Check the base edge for length. This part of the cover should finish 13.5cm from the floor, so trim if necessary. Remove cover and stitch the front panel in place

Above: When using patterned fabric, match the design on the centre of each cover piece all down the middle of the chair. The plain skirt has inverted pleats at each corner

75

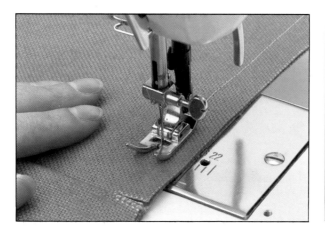

15 Face the back opening: cut a strip of fabric twice the length by 8cm. With right sides together, stitch the strip to the wrong side of the opening

16 Turn in 1.5cm along remaining raw edge of strip. Place fold to previous seamline on right side of cover. Stitch in place, then fold strip in half so it lies inside the cover

17 With right sides together, pin, tack and stitch skirt pieces together. At each end of skirt stitch a double 2.5cm hem. Repeat, to stitch a single 2.5cm hem along zigzagged base edge

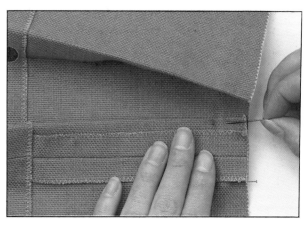

18 Fold the skirt into pleats, beginning in the centre of the skirt and working outwards both ways. Position any seams at the back of a pleat. Press

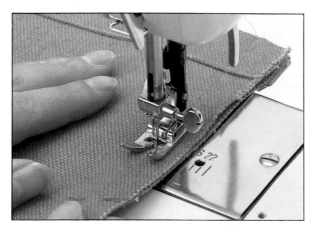

19 Place skirt to cover with right sides together, matching skirt ends to back opening edges. Taking 1.5cm seam allowance, pin, tack and stitch skirt to cover

20 Place cover over sofa and fold in opening edges. Mark positions of hooks and eyes, placing the last pair just below seamline of skirt. Stitch fastenings in place

Seat cushions

The covers for the seat and the back cushions on a sofa are made in the same way as square gusseted cushions (see pages 68-9). A zip is inserted in the centre of the back gusset so that the covers can be easily removed for washing. To calculate the amount of extra fabric you need for each cushion measure the cushion pad and follow page 68. If you prefer, the zip can be inserted in a concealed opening: place the back gusset pieces with right sides together; pin and tack together down the seamline. Position the zip, with the teeth centred, behind the tacked seam. Pin, tack and stitch the zip in place. Make up the cushions as pages 68-9; pipe the edges if desired.

Piping

All seams that outline the chair or sofa can be piped for added strength and a professional look. There should be enough room between the larger shapes on the cutting layout to cut the bias strips. If using a contrast fabric, choose one that is similar in weight and texture to the cover fabric. As a rough guide, you will need 12 metres of covered piping cord for a chair and 30 metres for a sofa. If the piping cord is not pre-shrunk, wash it before making up, as it can shrink by as much as 25 per cent. The piping cord is covered by 5cm-wide strips cut on the bias of the fabric between the larger pattern pieces. Join the strips together on the straight of grain. Complete piping and insert as pages 64-5.

Alternative skirt styles

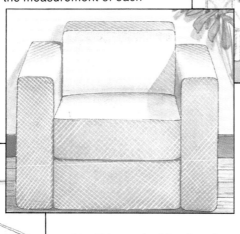

Below: For a tailored skirt, subtract measurements as given for the pleated skirt (see page 72). Measure the width of each side of the sofa, allowing 3cm for seam allowance, and cut an 18cm-wide piece of fabric to these four measurements, plus four 18cm-square inserts to make the corner pleats. Join skirt pieces together with right sides facing in this order: outside back, insert, outside arm, insert, front, insert, outside arm, insert. Make hems along base and short edges. Fold inserts to make inverted pleats and tack across top edges to secure. Stitch skirt to cover, matching pleats to corners.

Below: For a plain, tied-under cover follow the instructions for measuring up. Cut four strips 10cm wide by the measurement of each side. Trim each side of each strip to fit between the legs. Stitch a double 1cm hem on each short edge. Make a 3cm-wide casing along base edges. Stitch the top edge to the cover sides. Fit on cover. Cut a length of tape and thread through each casing. Pull up and tie. Push cord ends inside flaps.

Above: For a gathered skirt, subtract measurements given for the pleated skirt (see page 72). Cut out 18cm-deep strips which, when stitched together, will measure one and a half times the total distance round the sofa or chair. Turn a 1.5cm hem to wrong side on base and both short edges of the strip, neatening the raw edges. Work two rows of gathering stitches 1.5cm and 1cm from top edge of the strip. Divide up the base evenly and then divide the frill into the same number of sections. Pull up gathers, matching up each section in turn. Pin, tack and stitch frill in place.

Round cushions and bolsters

In any setting, round cushions suggest and give soft comfort.
Make them in various sizes, styles and fabrics and then group
them together for greater impact

Round cushion pads are available in a flat disc shape and a thicker version with a gusset. Both versions come in a range of sizes. The instructions show you how to make a plain round cover for a flat pad (the easiest to make), and a more decorative cover gathered into a central button. See illustration opposite for some ideas.

Bolster cushions are firm, and traditionally used at the end of a couch or tailored sofa, although they also make attractive bedroom cushions. The most common size of bolster pad is 45cm long with a 17cm diameter. The instructions (pages 83-4) show how to make a fitted cover with two circular end pieces and zip opening, or a more elaborate, but easy-to-make, cover cut in one piece and gathered at both ends into tassels.

How to make a round cushion

WHAT YOU NEED
1 Fabric for cushion cover
2 Round cushion pad
Plus: Cutting-out and small sewing scissors, tape measure, tacking and matching thread, dressmaker's pins, needles, paper for pattern, string, pencil, drawing pin, pinboard or large cork tile, household or craft/paper scissors

NOTE If a round cushion pad is unobtainable you can make your own following Steps 1–6 below. See page 53 for fabrics and fillings. Stitch all seams twice.

HOW TO WORK OUT YOUR QUANTITIES
The amount of fabric required will depend on the size of the cushion pad, the width of the fabric and whether it has a large motif which you wish to centre on the cushion. To calculate the cutting size of the pieces,

measure the cushion pad as described below and then plan the most economical way of arranging the pieces on the fabric. On plain fabrics or those with a small pattern repeat, two pieces can usually be cut side by side across the width. On fabrics with a large motif or pattern repeat you may need extra fabric to obtain two whole repeats.

HOW TO MEASURE YOUR CUSHION PAD
Using a tape measure, measure the diameter of the cushion pad (that is, through the centre of the circle) and add a 3cm seam allowance to give the cutting size. You will need two circles this size for each cushion cover. To ensure a good circle, make a paper pattern before cutting out in fabric. Halve cutting size to give radius needed for drawing the circle.

When making your own cushion pad, make up a pattern 1.5cm larger than the cushion cover, to give a plump cushion.

1 To make a pattern for the circular pieces, use craft scissors to cut a square of paper slightly larger than cutting size of circle. Fold into quarters

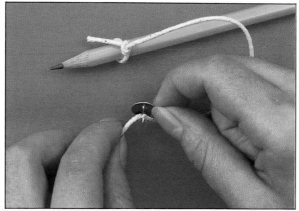

2 Cut a length of string 15cm longer than circle's radius. Tie one end round point of a pencil. Push drawing pin through opposite end so distance between equals radius

79

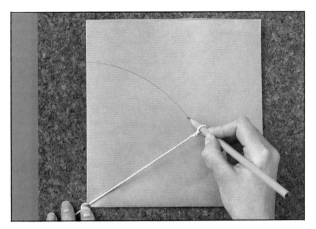

3 Place the folded paper on a pinboard or large cork tile and anchor the drawing pin at the folded corner. Holding the string taut, draw a quarter circle from edge to edge

4 Carefully cut along the pencil line, through all four thicknesses of paper. Open out to give the whole pattern and press perfectly flat with a cool iron

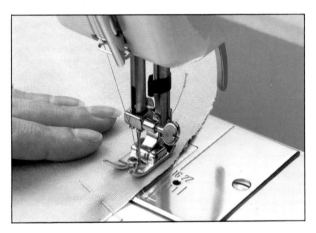

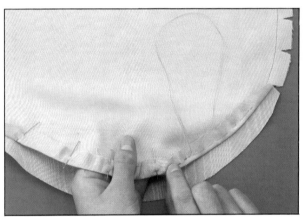

5 Using the pattern, cut out two pieces of fabric. Place right sides together. Pin, tack and stitch two-thirds of the way round the edge, taking a 1.5cm seam allowance

6 Notch the seam allowance all round the cover to give a good edge. Turn the seam allowance to the wrong side at both edges of the opening and tack in place

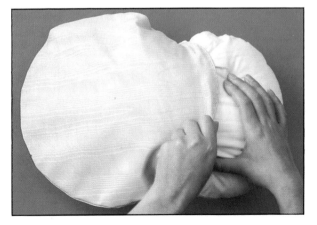

7 Turn the cushion cover through to the right side, bringing the seam right to the edge. Insert the cushion pad and slipstitch the opening closed

How to make a gathered cover

WHAT YOU NEED
1 Fabric for cushion cover
2 Round cushion pad
3 Two large self-covering buttons
Plus: Sewing materials as on page 79

HOW TO WORK OUT YOUR QUANTITIES
To calculate the cutting size of the two cushion pieces, measure the cushion pad as described on page 79. The fabric required will depend on the size of the cushion pad, the width of the fabric and the depth of the repeat (see page 79).

HOW TO MEASURE YOUR CUSHION PAD
This gathered cover is made from two rectangular pieces of fabric, both the same size. To calculate the cutting size, first measure the circumference of the cushion pad by placing a tape measure loosely around the edge. Measure the diameter across the centre of the cushion pad.

Add a 3cm seam allowance to the circumference to give the length of each of the two rectangular cushion pieces. Halve the diameter of the cushion pad and add a 3cm seam allowance to give width of each piece.

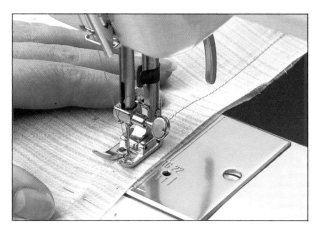

1 Cut out two rectangles of fabric to the required size. With right sides facing, pin, tack and stitch together along one long edge, taking 1.5cm seam allowance

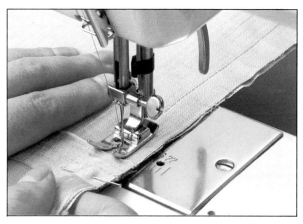

2 Press seam open. Then fold across length, right sides together, so short edges match. Pin, tack and stitch together, taking a 1.5cm seam allowance. Press seam open

3 Turn cover to the right side. Turn 1.5cm to the wrong side along each raw edge and tack. Make a row of 1cm-long gathering stitches by hand close to each folded edge

4 Pull up the gathering threads on one edge to bring the fabric together at the centre of the cover. Fasten off the ends securely by backstitching

81

5 Place the cushion pad inside the cover so the long seam on the cover sits on the edge of the pad. Pull up the gathering threads on the remaining edge and fasten off

6 Cover the two buttons in matching fabric. Stitch to the gathered centre at each side of the cushion to give a neat finish. Fasten off securely

How to make a plain bolster cover

WHAT YOU NEED
1 Fabric for bolster cover
2 Bolster cushion pad
3 Zip, 20cm shorter than bolster length
Plus: Sewing materials as on page 79, string, pencil, drawing pin, pinboard or large cork tile, craft/paper scissors

HOW TO WORK OUT YOUR QUANTITIES
The amount of fabric required will depend on the size of the bolster pad and the width of the fabric. Measure the bolster as right and calculate the cutting sizes of the pieces. Then work out the best way of cutting from the fabric.

HOW TO MEASURE THE BOLSTER PAD
Measure the length of bolster from the seam at one end to opposite seam. Measure the circumference of the bolster, placing the tape measure loosely around the cushion pad, and the diameter of the circular end.

For a bolster with circular end pieces, add a 3cm seam allowance to both the length and the circumference to give the cutting size for the rectangular bolster pieces. For the end pieces, add a 3cm seam allowance to the diameter to give the cutting size of the end, and halve this to give the radius needed for drawing the circular pattern (see page 79).

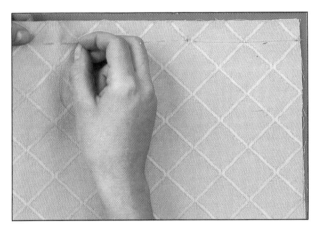

1 Fold the main piece in half, with right sides together and long edges together. Pin and tack 1.5cm from edge. Stitch in from each end, leaving an opening the length of zip

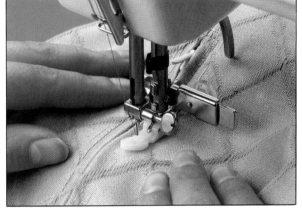

2 Press the seam open. Place zip face down over the tacked part of the seam, aligning the zip teeth with the seam. Fit zipper foot to machine and stitch zip in place

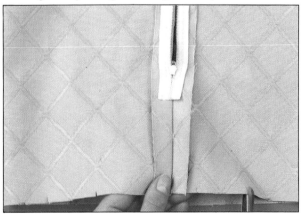

3 Using the paper pattern, cut out the two circular end pieces. Open the zip and clip into the seam allowance at each end of the main section of the bolster

4 Pin, tack and stitch the circular end pieces to the main piece, right sides together. Notch seam allowances. Turn right side out and insert the pad

83

How to make a decorative bolster cover

WHAT YOU NEED

1 Fabric for bolster cover
2 Bolster cushion pad
3 Two 18cm-long tassels
Plus: Sewing materials as on page 79

HOW TO WORK OUT YOUR QUANTITIES

This bolster cover is made from one rectangular piece of fabric. To calculate the cutting size, first measure bolster, (page 83). Add diameter of the circular end, plus 3cm, to the length of the bolster, to give the length of the rectangle. Add 3cm to the circumference to give the width.

1 Cut one piece of fabric to required size. Fold in half, wrong sides facing, long edges matching. Pin, tack and stitch with a French seam (page 41), taking 1.5cm allowance

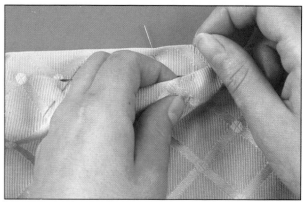

2 Turn the cover to the right side. Turn 1.5cm to the wrong side at each end. Pin and tack. Make a row of gathering stitches close to the folded edge at each end (see page 81)

3 Insert the bolster cushion pad centrally inside the cover. Pull up gathering thread at each end of the cover to bring the edges together and fasten off securely

4 Position the rosette of one tassel over one gathered end of the bolster and catchstitch in place. Repeat with the remaining tassel at the other end of the bolster

TABLE LINEN
Tablecloths and napkins

Rectangular or square tablecloths are very easy to make and
can transform a stark dining area or plain corner table

You can make a plain tablecloth in under an hour whether you have a sewing machine or want to do it by hand. Buy fabric specially (see below) or use remnants. If you have a left-over length of curtaining, create a matched effect for an undercloth, adding an easy-to-wash, co-ordinated top cloth to protect the main one at mealtimes. Use a heatproof cloth underneath to protect the table.

Your table may be too wide for you to be able to use one width of fabric. In this case don't just seam the cloth down the middle which would create an ugly central seam. Instead sew together pieces of mix and match fabrics that form their own design, or cut one width of fabric in half and sew to either side of centre panel. Alternatively, add a wide border of a different fabric mitring the corners for best results.

The basic cloth shown here is simply hemmed with neat mitred corners. Make a decorative bordered design or use it to cover the first as a small square overcloth with a lace and ribbon edging for extra decoration.

Sew simple napkins to match—remember to buy enough extra fabric—or you can use up fabric remnants.

Choosing fabrics and trimmings

Tablecloth fabrics must be washable, as meal times can be messy occasions, especially if you have a young family. And, if mixing and matching fabrics together, it is important that they are colourfast so that pale colours do not develop a coloured hue after laundering! Cotton and cotton mixtures are best, as they will stand up to everyday life. For a very simple no-sew cloth use spongeable PVC-coated fabric cut to size.

Try to pick trimmings that are compatible with the fabric, for example, cotton lace and ribbons for cotton fabrics, so that the trimmings can be washed in the same way as the fabrics and will not shrink to give a wavy edge. Make sure that the ribbon is colourfast too.

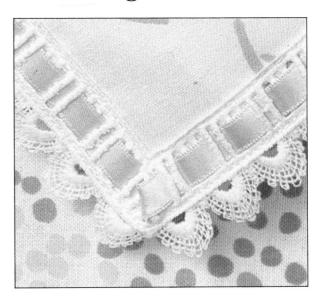

How to measure your table

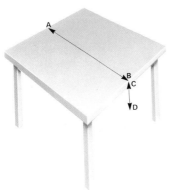

For a square table, measure the table across the top from one edge to the opposite edge A–B. Then you should add to this the required overhang C–D.

For a rectangular table, measure the length E–F and then the width of the table top from edge to edge G–H in the same way, adding the overhang to both measurements J–K

How to make a straight-sided tablecloth

WHAT YOU NEED

Fabric

Plus: Cutting-out and small sewing scissors, tacking and matching thread, pins, needles, tape measure

NOTE Check that your chosen fabric is washable, and colourfast. Pick a sewing thread that is compatible with your chosen fabric to avoid the possibility of either one shrinking disproportionately and causing unsightly puckering after laundering. Choose a colour that matches the background fabric.

HOW TO WORK OUT YOUR QUANTITIES

Measure the length and width of the table top (see opposite), picking the style of table you want to cover, then follow the measuring instructions for that table. Decide on the amount of overhang you want (20cm-30cm is ideal) and add the total overhang to the table measurement, plus 5cm for hems. If the total measurement is wider than the fabric, cut one centre panel and then cut one more length and cut it in half lengthways. Pin, tack and stitch each half length to either side of centre width with flat fell seams (see page 12).

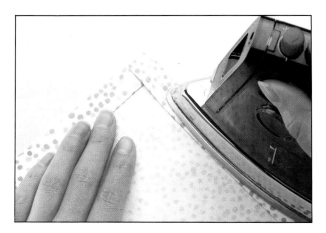

1 Cut out piece of fabric to the correct size. On each edge fold 1.5cm to the wrong side and press. Fold over a further 1.5cm and press. Open out the last hem fold

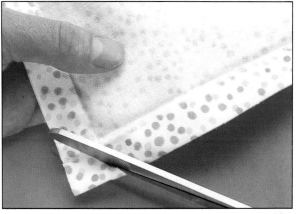

2 Cut across each corner to within 6mm of the inner corner point, cutting through the folded edges. Fold back the corners with right sides together matching cut edges and edges of fabric

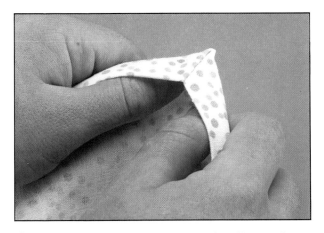

3 Pin and stitch the corners on the diagonal, 6mm from the raw edges stitching through the inner corner point. Press seams flat. Turn corners to right side

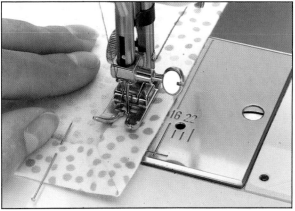

4 Fold under the double hem again along pressed edges. Pin, tack and stitch all round the outer edge of the tablecloth. Pull threads to wrong side and fasten off

Adding a decorative edge

WHAT YOU NEED
1 Fabric   3 Eyelet lace
2 Lace edging   4 Ribbon
Plus: Cutting-out and sewing scissors, thread, pins, needles, tape measure.

HOW TO WORK OUT YOUR QUANTITIES
For fabric follow instructions on page 87. For the lace and eyelet edgings, measure cloth outside edge, add 2cm for the corners. For an overcloth, position undercloth on table and decide on the overcloth size — it will look best if it overhangs the table.

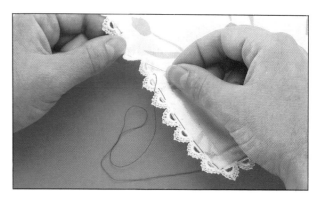

1 Cut out one fabric piece to required size. Turn single 1cm hem to right size. Pin and tack. Pin and tack lace to right side of cloth

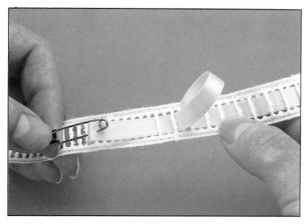

2 Take a length of ribbon and eyelet lace to fit round all four sides. Fold over 1cm of ribbon, fasten a safety pin through fold and weave the ribbon in and out of eyelet lace

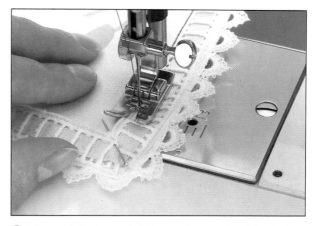

3 Pin and tack eyelet lace all round tablecloth, covering inner edge of lace and raw edge of fabric. Fold under excess at corners into mitres. Stitch to fit. Stitch along both edges

How to make table napkins

WHAT YOU NEED
Fabric
Plus: Cutting-out and small sewing scissors, tacking and matching thread, pins, needles, tape measure

HOW TO WORK OUT YOUR QUANTITIES
The most economical way of making napkins is to cut two fabric squares across the fabric width, so napkins are usually between 45cm and 50cm square. For tea-time use, make smaller napkins about 20cm square across width of the fabric.

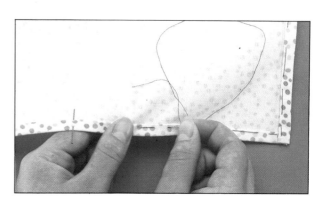

Cut out napkins to the required size. Fold a double 7mm hem folding neat corners. Pin, tack and stitch all round the napkin

Circular tablecloths

Make your own tablecloth to help protect your dining table, or add
a splash of colour to a room by covering a small display table

Circular tablecloths can be made to any size to suit your table. A cloth for a dining table should be fairly short so that the fabric will not get in the way of people's legs. Cover the cloth with a smaller overcloth.

A small display table looks best when covered with a floor-length cloth and, if you wish, a small over-cloth. The long cloth covers the table completely, so you can use an old, battered table or even make one from a round piece of chipboard.

Choose easy-care fabrics like polyester-cotton so that the cloth can be easily laundered. Wide-width fabrics such as sheeting are best when making a large cloth so that there is no need to join fabric widths. On narrower furnishing fabrics, it is a good idea to position half-widths on either side of the central panel.

How to measure your table

Using a tape measure or a retractable steel ruler, first measure the diameter of the table top (AB) — that is, the distance through the centre of the table. Then decide on the depth of the overhang (CD or CE), measuring from the table top downwards. Add a hem allowance to the overhang measurement. Double this total and add it to the diameter of the table top to find the overall diameter of the cloth. If you are unsure of the length of the overhang you want, make a complete circular pattern (see Steps 1–4, pages 79–80) and try it on the table to check whether the drop is the right length. Adjust if necessary. Remember that a dining tablecloth should have a short overhang to prevent the cloth tangling in people's legs.

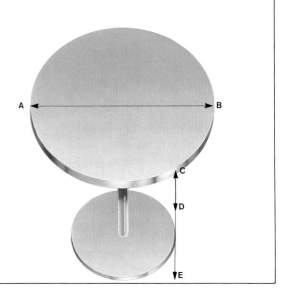

How to make a cloth from wide fabric

WHAT YOU NEED
1 Wide-width fabric such as sheeting
2 Large sheet of paper
3 Drawing pin
4 String
Plus: Cutting-out and small sewing scissors, matching and tacking threads, tape measure, pins, needle, pencil
NOTE If you use this tablecloth under a lace overcloth, try to match the pattern of the fabric to the lace — floral with floral, geometric with geometric.

HOW TO WORK OUT YOUR QUANTITIES
Measure the table-top (AB) as shown above. For a floor-length cloth, measure from the table edge to the floor (CE). Then decide on the depth of the hem — for a neat finish on a circular cloth, you must have a narrow hem — and add it to the diameter of the cloth. Deduct 1.5cm from this total so that the edge of the cloth will hang just above the floor. Any spare fabric can be used for table napkins (see page 88). If using lace fabric for napkins, bind the edges.

1 Make a pattern of one quarter of the tablecloth, as Steps 1 and 2, page 92. Fold fabric into four and using pattern, cut out cloth. Stitch all round cloth 1.5cm from outer edge

2 This stitching line marks the finished edge of the cloth. Set the iron to the correct temperature and press the outer edge to the wrong side along the stitched line

3 After pressing in the outer edge, carefully turn under the raw edge inside the hem, so hem is halved. Pin and tack round hem. Keep checking that the hem is the same all round

4 Using matching thread, stitch all round the outer edge of the tablcloth, close to the fold edge. Press round the outer edge of the tablecloth to finish

How to make a circular, lace overcloth

WHAT YOU NEED
1 Lace fabric
2 1.3cm-wide bias binding
3 Large sheet of paper
4 Drawing pin
5 String
Plus: Cutting-out and small sewing scissors, tacking and matching threads, tape measure, metre ruler, pins, needles, pencil
NOTE If the cloth is small, avoid a large pictorial design as this does not look good cut into a small area.

HOW TO WORK OUT YOUR QUANTITIES
Measure the table-top (AB) as opposite. Decide on the overhang (CD)—use a metre ruler as, with the stick standing beside the table, it will be much easier to visualize where the overcloth will hang. Alternatively, make up the undercloth first so you can see how much you want to display, and then decide on the overhang of the top cloth. For the binding, measure round the outer edge of the quarter pattern (see below) and multiply the measurement by four, adding 2cm for joining.

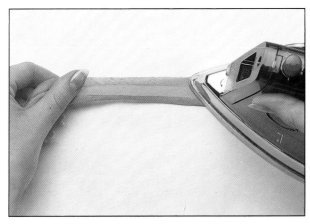

1 Make a pattern of one quarter of the tablecloth as Steps 1 and 2, page 92. Fold the lace into four and cut out, using the pattern. Unfold one edge of the bias binding and press

2 Place the unfolded flat edge of the bias binding all round the the wrong side of the tablecloth, matching the raw edges together. Stitch to tablecloth along crease line

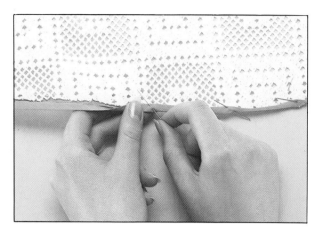

3 Fold binding in half on to the right side of the cloth over the raw edges of the lace. Pin the binding in place, checking that the bound hem is the same width all round the cloth

4 Tack and stitch binding in place all round the outer edge of the tablecloth close to the folded edge of the binding. To finish, carefully press round the bound edge

How to make a seamed, frilled cloth

WHAT YOU NEED
1 Furnishing fabric
2 Piping cord
Plus: Scissors, threads, pins, needles, tape measure, paper, string, pencil, drawing pin
NOTE When the fabric is too narrow to gain the correct size of the cloth, stitch two widths to either side of a central panel, but position the seams carefully so that you do not just add two narrow strips of fabric on either side of centre. Trim centre panel if necessary so side panels will be a reasonable width.

HOW TO WORK OUT YOUR QUANTITIES
Measure the table-top (AB) as page 90. Measure the overhang (CE) as for the cloth on pages 90-1. Decide on the depth of the frill and deduct this amount from the overhang measurement. Add the two measurements—the table top and overhang—together. If total is greater than the fabric width, double the fabric amount. For frill, allow for one and a half times the outer edge measurement by twice the depth, plus 3cm. For the piping cord, measure the outer edge.

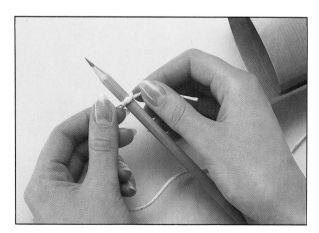

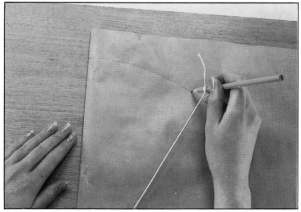

1 Cut a piece of paper slightly larger than a quarter of the tablecloth. Cut a length of string 15cm longer than cloth length from table centre. Tie one end of string round a pencil

2 Fasten pin through the other end of the string, with the string the exact length of cloth from table centre. Draw an arc across the paper. Cut along marked line

Choose a smart print fabric and make a floor-length cloth to cover a small circular display table. Finish the hem edge with self-covered piping and deep frill. Be economic and save fabric by cutting your frill widths from across the fabric width. The finished cloth should hang just above the floor

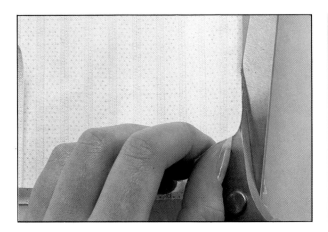

3 Cut two lengths of fabric to the required size. Fold one fabric length in half lengthways, carefully cut along the fold to form two half widths for side panels

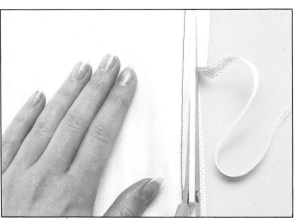

4 Position each half length to either side of complete fabric width, matching the pattern. Pin, tack and stitch together with flat fell seams (page 12), taking 1.5cm seam allowance

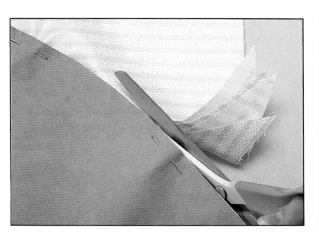

5 Fold fabric in half both ways, matching outer edges and seams. Position the pattern to fabric, matching centre points. Pin in place. Cut out following the pattern edge

6 Unfold fabric. Measure round the outer edge. For piping, cut 5cm-wide bias strips, which when stitched together will be the same length as the outer edge. Stitch strips together

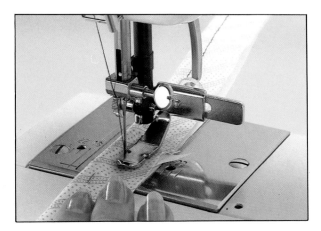

7 Place piping cord centrally to wrong side of bias strip. Fold strip in half round cord. Pin, tack and stitch down complete length using a piping or zipper foot on the sewing machine

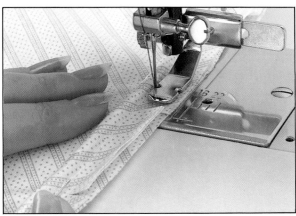

8 Snip into piping fabric at regular intervals all down length. Position covered piping cord round outer edge of tablecloth. Pin, tack and stitch using piping or zipper foot

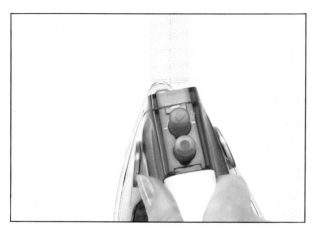

9 For the frill, cut out straight strips from across the fabric width. Join strips together into a ring, with plain seams. Press. Fold frill in half to form a double frill; pin and tack

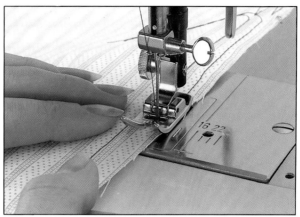

10 Divide the outer edge of the tablecloth into four and mark. Divide the frill ring into four and mark. Gather along each frill section 1.5cm and 1cm from raw edges

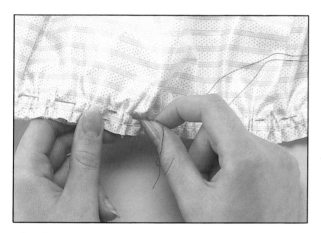

11 Match up marks on frill with marks on outer edge of cloth. Pull up gathering threads in each section of frill to fit. Pin, tack and stitch frill to cloth, using piping or zipper foot

12 Neaten the raw edges of frill and tablecloth: trim down the piping fabric; place frill and tablecloth edges together; zigzag stitch all round the outer edge

Decorative placemats

Show off a smart table top by using pretty placemats. Make them padded and they will protect your table from any surface damage

The great virtues of placemats are that they save on the washing and ironing of tablecloths and, at the same time, show off an attractive table which would otherwise be hidden by a cloth. They also provide a heat-resistant layer between hot plates and the table, are suitable for all kinds of surfaces and work particularly well on polished wood tables.

Placemats need first and foremost to be heat resistant. This can be achieved by sandwiching wadding between two layers of fabric.

Placemats can be made in rectangular, square, oval or circular shapes and those made with wadding can be quilted. Always ensure that the fabric, wadding and binding are all washable. Firm furnishing cottons are the best choice

of fabric, and they are available in a wide range of plain colours and patterns. By quilting together two co-ordinating fabrics you can make reversible placemats. Pre-quilted fabrics with different patterns on each side are ideal for this and will save you quilting your own. Wipe-clean mats made in PVC-coated cotton are another alternative, ideal for children.

In some cases, wadding-filled mats will not be sufficiently heat resistant, for instance, against very hot casseroles. Ordinary cork mats can be enclosed in a decorative removable cover which will look pretty on the table whilst performing this essential protective function. To complete the setting, napkins can be made to match the placemats.

How to make a rectangular mat

WHAT YOU NEED

1 Main fabric
2 White cotton fabric
3 Medium-weight polyester wadding
4 13mm wide bias binding

Plus: Cutting-out and small sewing scissors, tape measure, tacking and matching thread, dressmaker's pins, needles, ruler, pair of compasses, chalk and pencil.

HOW TO WORK OUT YOUR QUANTITIES

A rectangular mat 45cm wide×30cm deep will take a standard dinner plate and cutlery. For each mat you will need two pieces of fabric plus one piece of wadding, all cut to the finished size. Draw a rough cutting layout on paper. Remember that fabrics with a one-way design should be cut so the pattern runs in the same direction on each mat. If the fabric has a large motif, allow a whole pattern repeat for each piece. If making matching napkins allow extra fabric, see page 88. For the amount of bias binding needed measure round outer edge and add 3cm overlap, then multiply by the number of mats/napkins.

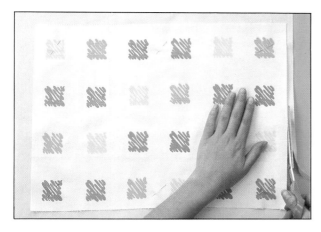

1 For each mat, cut out one rectangle the required size in the main fabric, centring the pattern. Also, cut out one rectangle in backing fabric and one in wadding

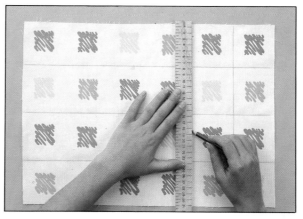

2 Mark quilting lines lightly on main fabric using tailor's chalk or a hard pencil and a ruler. Follow regular lines or intervals in the pattern, or mark lines 3.5cm apart

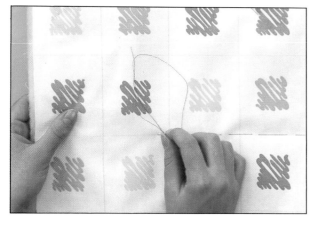

3 Sandwich wadding between the two fabrics, with wrong sides of fabrics inside. Pin and tack together in both directions along central marked quilting lines and then around the edges

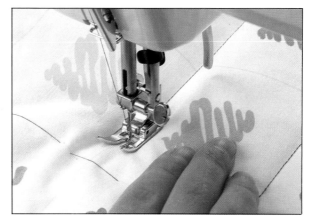

4 Quilt the three layers together with a medium-length stitch, following the marked lines. Begin at centre and work outwards, stitching shorter rows on the rectangle first

97

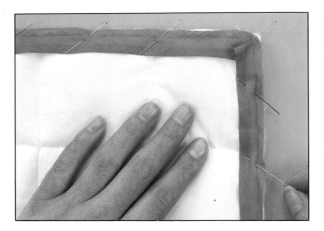

5 Unfold one side of binding. Position unfolded side to back of mat, matching edges together. At each corner neatly fold the binding into a mitre. Pin binding in place

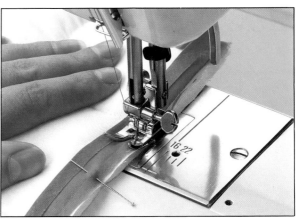

6 Stitch binding in place through outer fold in binding. Begin each side of stitching at corner and end at opposite corner point, so corners can be folded into mitres

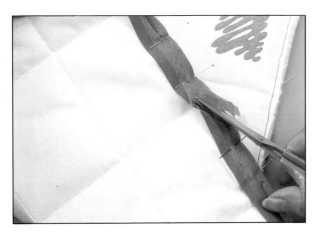

7 Where binding ends meet, unpin the ends, place right sides together and join on the straight grain with a plain seam. Trim seam. Complete stitching round binding

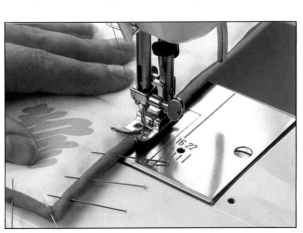

8 Fold binding over edge to right side of mat. Pin all round, tucking in each corner into a mitre. Topstitch close to the inner edge of the binding all round mat

How to make an oval mat

WHAT YOU NEED
1 Two co-ordinating fabrics
2 Medium-weight polyester wadding
Plus: Sewing equipment, see page 97.

HOW TO WORK OUT YOUR QUANTITIES
An oval placemat 45cm wide × 30cm deep
will take a standard dinner plate and cutlery.
The best way to ensure a good shape is to
make a paper pattern (Steps 1 and 2 below).
For each mat you will need one piece of each
of the two co-ordinating fabrics and one piece
of wadding, all cut to the finished size of the

mat. Before buying the fabric, work out the
most economical way of cutting the pieces.
For the binding: To calculate how much extra
fabric is required, first find the length of
binding needed for one placemat by
measuring round the edge of the pattern and
add 3cm for joining. Multiply this length by
the number of mats you are making to find
the total length of binding required. For a
13mm-wide binding, cut bias strips 23mm
wide and as long as possible to minimize
joins. Stitch strips together on the straight
grain to make up the length required.

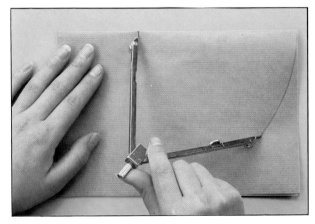

1 Cut a rectangle the required size in paper.
Fold into four. Mark 15cm in along fold line.
Set compasses to 15cm. With point on mark
draw an arc from outer edge to curve corner

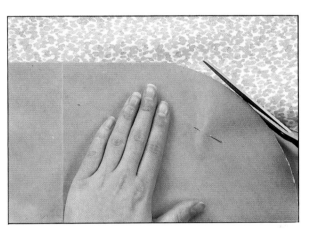

2 With paper folded, cut along marked line.
Unfold pattern and use this to cut out one
piece in each of the two co-ordinating fabrics.
Cut one piece in wadding

3 Sandwich wadding between two fabrics.
Quilt round outline of centre motifs. For
binding, cut bias strips and join to make
required length. Press 5mm in along each edge

4 Pin and stitch binding round back of mat,
joining ends together at centre of one
straight edge to fit, Steps 5 to 8, opposite. Fold
binding to right side and slipstitch to finish

99

DECORATIVE PLACEMATS

Above: Protect your table with a quilted tablemat. For a co-ordinated look, choose a bold print for the mat and bind the edges with a matching small-print fabric, which can also be used to make the napkins

Left: Sandwich the wadding between the two co-ordinated fabrics and tack together. Quilt only round the main central motifs. Quilt round the flower centres too, so on the reverse side of the mat you have reverse outlines of the flowers

How to make patchwork placemats

Patchwork placemats are a lovely way to brighten up your meals, and can also be used as cheerful tray mats as shown in our photograph. Traditionally, patchwork is sewn by hand (see pages 59-61), but it can also be done by machine, without paper templates, for a much quicker result. (This same method may be used for hand-sewing the patches together.)

The step by step instructions on pages 102-3 show you how to make up the patchwork fabric, then you can proceed as for the quilted mats on pages 96-8. If desired, instead of binding the edges, fold under a 1cm seam allowance and top-stitch, leaving a 3cm gap; hand-sew piping cord round the edges, tucking the ends into the gap and hand-sewing to close.

WHAT YOU NEED

1 Card in 2 different colours for templates
2 Fabrics in 5 different colourways
3 White paper or graph paper for design
4 Craft knife
5 Steel ruler
6 Felt-tip pens or coloured pencils
7 Card to cut on
Plus: Cutting-out scissors, pins, fine sewing needle, tacking thread and sewing thread to tone with fabrics, soft pencil

HOW TO WORK OUT YOUR QUANTITIES

Do this after the design has been finalized and the templates made. For smaller patchworks, place the templates—which include seam allowances—over the appropriate fabric to check you have enough. For larger patchworks, count the number of patches needed and make a plan showing the dimensions (right). Add up the dimensions to give the width and depth. When planning, bear in mind the width of the fabric available and lay out the patches economically. You cannot work out quantities in this way when you are using window templates.

Piecing diagram for tablemat

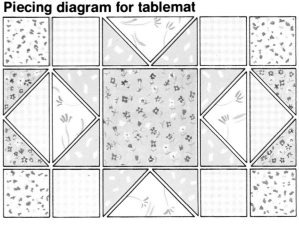

Altogether there are 27 patches comprising 1 large square, 8 small squares (4 each in two colourways), 12 small triangles (4 of one colour and 8 of another), 6 large triangles (4 of one colour and 2 of another). Join together in sequence shown above

1a **Using coloured pens:** Plan your design and draw outline to actual size where possible. Fill in shapes with the pens to test different colour combinations, *or*

1b **Using fabric scraps:** Cut off scraps from the fabrics you would like to use. Draw outline of the design and fill in shapes with scraps. Test fabrics in different positions

2 Make two templates for each shape: one to include a 1cm seam allowance and one the actual size of the finished patch. Use a different coloured card for each type

3 Using the large templates and working on the wrong side of the fabric, draw round the first shape. Butt template up to drawn lines for the next patch to avoid waste

4 On motif patterns, use a window template. Move it around until a suitable area shows. Lightly draw round inner sewing line and outer line which includes seam allowance

5 Cut out the shapes from the various fabrics. Refer to your plan to ensure you have cut the right amount from each fabric. Keep each colour and shape in a separate pile

6 Centre the smaller solid template over the cut-out shape and draw round with pencil on wrong side of fabric. This is your sewing line. Keep the pencil very sharp

7 Right sides together, pin the triangles in pairs, matching the sewing lines. If you wish, tack along line and remove pins. Check position of patches against your plan

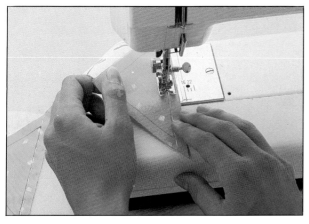

8 Machine stitch the pairs together along sewing line. Remove tacking stitches, if any, and press seam to one side, preferably over to the darker patch

9 Continue joining patches, pressing seam before adding next patch. Join smaller patches, then combine to make larger units. Trim corners. Complete steps 1-8, pages 97-8.   103

INDEX

Picture credits
Simon Butcher: 59, 60, 61, 102, 103; Ray Duns: 14, 15, 16, 31, 32, 33, 34, 35, 50, 51; Bruce Hemming: 42, 44(t&c); Tony Hurley: 10, 11, 13, 29, 49, 70, 71, 75(br), 96, 97, 98, 100; Michael Murray: 17, 36, 39, 41(b), 45, 46, 52, 53, 101(b); Roger Payling: 7, 9, 18, 19, 20, 21, 27, 28, 30, 37, 38, 40, 41(t), 47, 48, 87, 88, 90, 91, 92, 94, 95; Spike Powell: 6; John Russell: 23; Kim Sayer: 24, 85, 86; Steve Tanner: 22, 25, 43, 44(b), 54, 55, 56, 57, 58, 63, 64, 65(t), 66, 67, 68(t), 69(t), 73, 74, 75(t&l), 76, 79, 80, 81, 82, 83, 84, 99; Jerry Tubby: Front cover, 62, 65(b), 68-9(b), 78, 89, 93, 95(b).
Illustrations by Berry/Fallon Design: 26, 32, 46, 72, 86, 90; Tony Grahame: 8; Bill Le Fever: 12, 69, 77; Chris Lyon: 102.